THE COUNTRY RHYMES OF
SAMUEL THOMSON

THE BARD OF CARNGRANNY
1766 - 1816

THE FOLK POETS OF ULSTER

TITLES IN THE SERIES

VOLUME ONE
THE COUNTRY RHYMES OF
HUGH PORTER
THE BARD OF MONEYSLANE

VOLUME TWO
THE COUNTRY RHYMES OF
JAMES ORR
THE BARD OF BALLYCARRY

VOLUME THREE
THE COUNTRY RHYMES OF
SAMUEL THOMSON
THE BARD OF CARNGRANNY

PRETANI PRESS

VOLUME THREE
THE FOLK POETS OF ULSTER

THE COUNTRY RHYMES OF

SAMUEL THOMSON

THE BARD OF CARNGRANNY
1766 - 1816

INTRODUCED BY
ERNEST McA SCOTT & PHILIP ROBINSON

First published by Pretani Press, 1992
78 Abbey Street, Bangor BT20 4JB

Introduction copyright ©
Ernest McA Scott & Philip Robinson

This book has received financial assistance under
the Cultural Traditions Programme which aims to
encourage acceptance and understanding of
cultural diversity.

Design and typesetting by Pegasus Design Consultants, Belfast.
Photography by Gemini, Belfast.
Antiques supplied by Robert Huffam, Carrickfergus.
Original maps by Alison Hogg.
Printed in Northern Ireland by
W & G Baird Limited, The Greystone Press, Antrim

ISBN 0 948868 19 8

PRETANI PRESS

CONTENTS

vii   The folk poets of Ulster

ix   Introduction

xviii   Subscribers' Names 1793, 1799 and 1806

1   To a Hedgehog

3   On a Spider

5   The Hawk and Weazle, a fable

6   Elegy, Lizie's Lament for her dog Lion

8   A Peripatiae

11   Bawsey's Elegy, and epitaph - on seeing her skull in a ditch

13   To the Cuckoo

15   The Unfortunate Fiddler

16   Jamie's Drone

18   The Country Dance

23   The Simmer Fair

27   Sonnet, written on Monday, July the first, old stile, 1802, being Templepatrick Fair-day, that year

28   The Roughfort Fair, a rustic parody on Gray's Elegy

33   Lyle's Hill - A Rhapsody, inscribed to Damon

38   Crambo Cave, To Damon

40   The Fairy Knowe: or, Damon's birth place

42   November, To Damon

44   Acrostic - To Damon

45   A Jonsonian Fragment, occasioned by a visit to Mr Burns, in Spring, 1794

47   Lines from Damon

49   Epistle to L[uke] M[ullan], a brother bard

53   Epistle to Mr R[ober]t B[urn]s

56   Lines, addressed to the Rev J[ames] P[orter]

57   Verses, composed in the hermitage of Greenmount, Sept. 3rd, 1801, addressed to Mrs Thomson

60   Templepatrick's address to the Right Honourable my L[or]d T[empleto]n

62	To Captain M'Dougall, Castle-upton, with a copy of the author's poems
64	Epistle to the Rev James Glass, MA
67	Answer, to Paine's "Age of Reason"
69	Elegy on R—— I——
71	Epistle to Mr R——, Belfast; on receiving a flattering epistle from him
74	To the Same
77	To a Blockhead - at school
78	John Cricket
80	On the death of a taylor
81	Willy sings Grizzy's Awa (Song)
83	Willy's farewell to whiskey
86	Davie and Sawney, an ale-house ecologue
93	Listen Lizie, lilting to tobacco
98	Postscript, with a pound of snuff
99	Elegy, to my Auld Coat
100	Elegy, to my Auld Shoen
102	The Bonnet - a poem, addressed to a Reverend miser
109	To my Boortree, written at the desire of the Rev Mr C——
111	Verses, on the assassination of a favourite thorn
113	Pastoral Elegy, to a favourite thorn, on its being cut down
115	Simkin, or a bargain's a bargain - a tale
118	Song
120	Epitaphs, on A B——
120	on Sarah B——
120	on a pedlar
121	on a gude fellow
121	on auld Josie
121	on J—— D——
121	on a remarkable little, ill-favour'd body
122	Epigram
122	Epigram, to a reading preacher
123	Lines composed for a stone, intended to be placed in front of the Rev John Paul's new Meeting House, now building in Carnmoney, 1806.

THE FOLK POETS OF ULSTER

The vernacular poetical tradition in Ulster was part of a much broader literary movement focussed in Scotland and culminating in the work of Robert Burns at the end of the eighteenth century. This virile Ulster tradition, much of it written in lowland Scots, has its beginnings early in the eighteenth century, before the work of Burns.

The works produced by the writers in this tradition were rescued by the late John Hewitt, in his book *Rhyming Weavers* (first published in 1974). This caused the value of these poets to be recognised by local historians, giving as they do a peasant's eye view of local life and customs, attitudes to religion and politics and such matters.

The purpose of this series is not to interpret or explain the poems, but to make them accessible once more, and to provide for each poet a biographical sketch. Some, nearly all, of the original volumes are extremely rare, and only found in the larger scholarly libraries.

Where the poets were prolific and produced several volumes, a selection has been made which prefers those written in Ulster-Scots rather than standard English, and which cover themes of local and historical interest.

The main era of publication was from c.1790 to c.1840, in the immediate wake of Burns' first edition of 1786, and during this period dozens of Ulster poets (notably from the counties of Down and Antrim) produced volumes of verse, mainly supported by subscriptions (pre-publication orders), overwhelmingly from friends and neighbours.

The vigorous Ulster-Scots of these poets will be difficult reading for even fluent speakers of modern vernacular. It is recommended that in reading those poems the full depth of meaning will not be transmitted unless a dialect dictionary (e.g. *The Concise Scots Dictionary*) is used frequently - even for those words which look familiar.

Series Editors:
J. R. R. Adams
P. S. Robinson

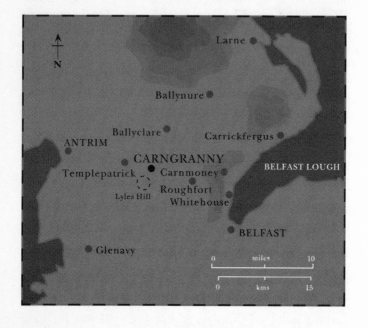

INTRODUCTION

Samuel Thomson was born in 1766 on the northern slopes of Lyle's Hill, at Carngranny near Templepatrick. He lived there for half a century in a small thatched cottage, despite a visit from Lord Templeton (his landlord and literary patron) in 1803, who hoped to find him a bigger house. Although he never became wealthy, as a lonely poet and child-less 'hedge' schoolmaster he was always able to entertain a wide circle of intellectual friends. Under the same roof he held court to well-known visiting radicals, wrote his poems and struggled to bring some fairly uninspiring pupils to higher standards of literacy. Such was his frustration at times as a teacher that in one poem addressed 'To a blockhead - at school', he wrote:

> *'Why thus yourself puzzle 'bout Latin and Greek,*
> *When English you neither can read, write, nor speak?*
> . . .
> *Tho' faith I would rather advise, as a neighbor,*
> *Quit books altogether, and strike up with labor,*
> *Shake hands with a shovel; a dunghill you'll find,*
> *A subject congenial at once to your mind'.*

Thomson called his house 'Crambo Cave' to express his own station in life as a rural bard. 'Crambo' was a popular parlour game of the day, where the skill was for each participant to compose, turn about, rhyming lines of verse. 'Crambo verse' became a by-word for doggerel poems, and in South Antrim 'Crambo Cave' became a focal point for a remarkable renaissance of vernacular Scots poetry in Ulster. In many ways, Samuel Thomson was the father of this re-awakened interest in Ulster-Scots poetry, although he was only 27 when his first book of poems was published in 1793. This volume was called *'Poems on Different Subjects, partly in the Scottish Dialect'*, and appeared six years after Burns' first volume. It was the earliest volume of collected poems published by any of the Ulster folk poets. Of course, poems written in broad Scots were being published (usually in newspapers or as broadsheets) long before Burns' time in both Ulster and Scotland, but this period began an outstanding revival marked by a succession of Ulster poets issuing books of their own collected works.

Thomson had the advantage over many of his brother-bards. They were self-taught 'rhyming weavers', while Thomson was a schoolmaster with pretensions as a classical scholar. When the United Irishmen were formed in Belfast in 1791, Thomson associated more with the intellectual leadership than with the less refined but equally rebellious rural peasantry. He published poems in the United Irishmen's radical newspaper, the *Northern Star,* from its establishment in 1792 until it was closed by the authorities in 1797. Indeed he was the most regular contributor throughout the period to the paper's poetic column, (the 'Muses Retreat'), even if he rarely wrote on specifically political themes. In one poem published in 1797 'To the Cuckoo', he included the following verse in the *Northern Star* version:

> *Sweet bird, exulting, sing aloud,*
> *Thru' every green wood, glade and glen,*
> *No more thou meet'st a **quarrelling crowd***
> *But TRUE UNITED IRISHMEN!*

These lines were omitted from the same poem when it was included in his second volume of poems, published in 1799, one year after the failed rebellion of 1798. In 1791 he wrote a poem dedicated as an 'Epistle to L- M-, a brother bard'. This was Luke Mullan, a neighbour from Roughfort who also was to contribute poems for the *Northern Star.* Luke Mullan's name appears in the list of subscribers to Thomson's first volume, but he became a more active United Irishman and fell from prominence after the rebellion. Thomson's radical politics can only be assumed from the friendships he made, and not by any direct political comment in his poems. Usually his poems were on everyday themes, in Scots, but occasionally his verses soared ostentatiously towards classicism. When the '98 rising failed, Thomson quickly modified his position and began to contribute to the less radical *Belfast News-letter.*

It is possible that Thomson simply saw himself as a writer adjusting to a rapidly changing political world, unlike some of his contemporaries who used their writings for political effect. On the other hand, Thomson may have been intimidated by the execution of his close friend, Rev James Porter, in 1798. Porter was a Presbyterian minister in Greyabbey, County Down, and was a leading intellectual among the Belfast radicals. He held public lectures there between 1795 and 1797 on astronomy and science, and wrote scathing political satires about landlordism in the Ards which were serialised in the *Northern Star*. In a letter to Thomson that Porter had written just before his arrest in 1798, he seemed to anticipate that he was going to have to pay for his outspokenness. In Thomson's 1799 volume, he included a poem he had written in 1798: 'Lines Addressed to the Rev J.P., Inclosing the foregoing'. The 'foregoing' was Thomson's poetic tribute to Robert Burns, and the poem to Porter began: 'With Scientific eye, exploring space', and ends with the line 'Of him who boasts that he can call you friend'.

When Thomson wrote his poems for the *Northern Star*, he often used a pseudonym. 'The Bards Farewell' (1793), 'Sonnet to Sleep' (1793) and 'Song on the Return of Spring' (1793) were simply signed *'Carngranny'*. Other poems over the next few years were contributed under the names of *S Thomson, Lyle; Thomalin, Lyle's Hill; S.T., Carngranny; 'Lyle'; Mathias Bramble, Lyle; Spur, Carngranny; Alexis, Carngranny; Colinet, Carngranny; Samuel Thomson, Carngranny; Thirsin, Carngranny; Immerito, Carngrannis; and Colin Clout, Carngranny.*

Besides Porter (who contributed prose rather than poetry) and Luke Mullan, there were two other literary contributors to the *Northern Star* with whom Samuel Thomson seemed to be on familiar terms: Rev James Glass and 'Albert' of Coleraine. Neither of these appear to have written much in Scots, and as far as Glass was concerned, his poetry was written in lengthy 'epic' style on subjects like 'Address to the Patriots of Belfast'. In 1792 Glass also published his 'Address to Mr Paine, Author of the Rights of

Man'. Paine's radical writings were influential and popular in the 1790s, but only among the intellectual leadership of the United Irishmen. His atheistic republicanism ruffled many feathers among the Presbyterian rank and file, and Thomson cared little for Paine's views. One unrestrainedly conservative poem, 'Answer To Paine's "Age of Reason"', reveals more political passion from Thomson than in any other poem he had written for the *Northern Star* before 1798. He had even reacted against the political content of Glass's poems, and in his 'Address to Rev James Glass, M.A.', he advised:-

> *O, sir, quat politics an' news!*
> *To other themes invoke your muse;*
> *Sic as by Leven's side*
> *Ance streekit on the downy grass ...*

In a subsequent issue of the *Northern Star*, Glass duly obliged with a mechanical Scots poem 'The Yellow-Haired Lassie', - a very inferior version of Burns' 'The Yellow-Haired Laddie.' Thomson had dedicated his 1793 volume to 'Mr Robert Burns, the Ayrshire poet', and in 1794 he journeyed to Dumfries to meet and exchange poems with Burns. In 'A Jonsonian fragment', he describes his journey and meeting, and refers to being accompanied by 'an only friend, Damon'. Damon (the Classical 'perfect friend' of Greek mythology) was the pseudonym Thomson used for a very dear and close friend: John Williamson of Carngranny. Many of his published poems were inscribed to Damon (such as 'Lyle's Hill, a Rhapsody', and 'Crambo Cave'). In one particular poem, 'Acrostic', he alternates the initial letters of the two friends' names (Samuel Thomson and John Williamson) to begin each line of the poem. The line beginning with T (for Thomson) explains: 'The reader here our names enwarp'd will find'. At the end of 'Crambo Cave' we find the lines:

> *The rustic owner doth solicit YOU*
> *To come and see him oft in CRAMBO CAVE.*
> *And chiefly DAMON, warmest heart of all,*
> *Thy cheerful company he'd often crave ...*

Similarly, at the end of 'The Fairy Knowe, or Damon's birth place' (which describes a visit to a desolate ruin at the site of Williamson's father's house), almost over-familiar sentiments are again expressed:

> *So Damon dear this verse is thine*
> *And thine its Author too.*

Many of Thomson's friends and brother-bards answered his poetic epistles in stanzas of their own, but only one poem has been included in this selection which is not from Thomson's own hand. This is the poem 'Lines from Damon', where we obtain a fleeting glimpse of Thomson's favourite protégé:

> *O Sam, thou learn'd me first to mark*
> *The dancing glow o' Burns's fire*
> *And gied to me that dainty spark*
> *That mak's me ay his sangs admire.*

Another poet whom Thomson corresponded in verse with was 'Albert of Coleraine', the *alias* of Alexander Kemp. When Albert was writing sonnets for the *Belfast News-letter*, Thomson would reply in similar vein, using the name 'Alexis'. Although Albert did not write in Scots himself, he published Burns' 'Address to the toothache' in the *Belfast News-letter* in 1797, claiming in a note that Burns had dictated the poem to him personally when he ('Albert') had visited the bard several years before.

Undoubtedly, Thomson saw himself as more than just an educated peasant. Although he had genuine fellow-feeling for the Presbyterian peasant-intellectuals of his own generation, he seems to have been a conservative at heart. He encouraged James Orr of Ballycarry to publish, first in the *Northern Star* and then in the *Belfast News-letter*, but by 1806 Orr had developed enough self confidence to write to Thomson, criticising some of his poems as being too Calvinist for his own taste, and in a poetic epistle, Orr strongly rebuked Thomson for seeking landlord patronage. The letter may have been simply a matter of Orr teasing

Thomson, for they both went occasionally to 'Covenanting' Presbyterian services. On one occasion they went together to take communion at Rev John Paul's new Covenanters' meeting house at Carnmoney. Thomson had composed a few lines to be inscribed on a stone for the front of the church, and the Rev Paul's home church was at Loughmourne, only a few miles from Orr.

Like Orr, Thomson saw no patriotic conflict in his Irish and Scots identities. They both praised 'Erin' at every opportunity, and saw themselves as Scots too. The northern flavour to their Irishness was expressed by the frequent use of the adjective 'Norland'. In his poem 'To Captain M'Dougall', Thomson reveals more of his own attitude:

> *I love my native land, no doubt,*
> *Attach'd to her thro' thick and thin*
> *Yet tho' I'm IRISH all WITHOUT,*
> *I'm every item SCOTCH WITHIN.*

Thomson's literary skill in Scots was quite remarkable. He could sustain lengthy Scots dialogue in his own Ulster-Scots, and imitate the Scots style of others. In 'A Pastoral, inscribed to my rhyme-composing brother, Mr Alexander Kemp' (Albert of Coleraine), Thomson produced an epic of almost 1000 lines which included lengthy portions of verse in the style and language of Burns, Allan Ramsay, Robert Fergusson and Dr James Beattie. He also displayed a somewhat pretentious classicism in other lengthy pastorals, all of which are unfortunately too long and of insufficient local interest to justify inclusion in this book. He claimed to have read Homer 'in translation only', along with Virgil, Horace, Milton, Young and Gay:

> *Auld Spencer, Pope and Dryden thro',*
> *Sweet Thompson, Shenstone, Goldsmith, Gray*

The second volume of Thomson's poems was published in 1799: *New Poems on a variety of different subjects*. This book, like the first, predated any other publication of collected

works by his contemporary poets in Ulster. Like the
previous volume, it contained many short Ulster-Scots
poems on subjects of every-day life and local events in
south Antrim. Many of these poems had also been
published in the *Belfast News-Letter* or in the *Northern Star*. In
1806 his third and final volume was published, *'Simple
Poems on a few Subjects'*. By this time he was beginning to
lose the cutting edge that had set the new generation of
Ulster poets apart as 'bards'– spokesmen for their own
rural communities. James Orr of Ballycarry, once a
'humble' contributor to the *Northern Star* and *News-Letter*
under Thomson's watchful eye, had by 1806 become
confident enough (with a volume of his own behind him)
to criticise Thomson's latest offerings openly. This criticism
was of the content rather than style of the works, but Orr
was also upset that Thomson did not keep on cool, distant
terms with the landlord class. The 1793 volume was
dedicated to 'Mr Robert Burns, the Ayrshire Poet', but the
1799 *'New Poems'* was inscribed to 'Samuel Thomson,
Esquire of Greenmount', apparently on no other motive
than the 'similarity of our names'. The dedicatory preface
is revealing.

> *...the Fates have unluckily placed me, wrestling with
> Fortune in a low station, I long since was an admirer of
> that INDEPENDENT SPIRIT which has distinguished
> THE FAMILY OF THE THOMPSONS, of
> GREENMOUNT.*

The 1806 book of *'Simple Poems'* had an even higher social
level as the object of its dedication: 'To the Right
Honourable Lord Viscount Templetown' (of
Templepatrick). By seeking landlord patronage, Thomson
may have been seen by some as having forfeited his
'bardship' of the rural peasantry. However, the subscribers'
lists for for each of his three volumes reveal no such shift in
his readership. The first two volumes attracted about 300
subscribers to each, while the 1806 volume had about 600.
It is remarkable that these subscribers were almost all
ordinary local people from his immediate locality, but very
few names occur on more than one list.

Thomson died in 1816 at the age of 50. He had lived to see a remarkable revival of folk poetry written in Ulster-Scots, and must have taken considerable pleasure in knowing that he had been in the vanguard of this movement. However, always uncomfortable with radical excesses (if not with politics altogether), Thomson never really achieved the status of *vox populi* that others were beginning to enjoy. The strength of his bardship rested almost entirely on his literary sophistication in both English and Scots, but the case ought not to be overstated. His poems on 'The Country Dance' and 'The Simmer Fair' give us a strong flavour of country life in South Antrim during the 1790s. Thomson was a serious man, but his poems had their humorous side too. In 'The Bonnet' he describes seeing a local clergyman stride out wearing a woman's bonnet, while he manages to evoke a real sense of drama and domestic comedy in 'Davie and Sawney, an ale-house ecologue'.

Almost 30 years after Thomson's death, one of the next generation of weaver-poets wrote a poetic testimonial to him. This 25-stanza tribute was from the pen of Robert Huddleston, the 'Bard of Moneyreagh' in county Down, who included an 'Elegy, to the Memory of the amiable and departed Thompson, Rural Bard, Carngranny' in his 1844 *Collection of Poems and Songs on Rural Subjects* . Among the many reasons Huddleston found to lament Thomson's lack of recognition was his unmarked grave in county Antrim:

> *O must it be? and shall he lie*
> *Without a garland for to bind*
> *His brows - or cypress to be nigh,*
> *Or holly rustling in the wind?*
> *'Thout aught to mark the desert waste,*
> *That we his lowly grave might find -*
> *O, must he sleep the lonely guest,*
> *To dark Obscurity resign'd?*

Although Huddleston had never met Thomson, he saw much to admire in his poems. Indeed, he seems to have seen certain parallels with his own frustrated ambitions:

Rear'd 'neath the lowly, humble roof,
Obscure to all but want and woe;
A kin to penury and the Muse -
Tho' distance great 'tween high and low,
So high the fence, thus fortune scoft,
Yet doom'd his airy wings to try;
Tho' caged the bird, he soared aloft,
And warbled forth mellodious joy.

At the end of this lengthy homage, Huddleston penned his own epitaph for Thomson:

Stap traveller awee, be weepin',
Beneath this turf lies Thompson sleepin';
Lean light upon his fousted banes,
And honour pay his dear remains.

O' Bards tho' mony he had brithers,
An' tae the pimps' and critics' swithers;
War't my vote tae decide the matter,
Than rura' Tamson devil a better.

ERNEST SCOTT
PHILIP ROBINSON

SUBSCRIBERS' NAMES
1793, 1799, 1806.

(These three lists have been alphabetically merged into a single list.)

A

72nd. Regiment, county Louth. 2
copies. 1806.
Adams, James, Doagh. 1806.
Adgey, Robert, Roughfort. 1806.
Adgie, James, Killead. 1806.
Agnew, John, Loughermore. 1806.
Alexander, Alexander, Belfast.
1793.
Alexander, James, jun., Belfast.
1806.
Alexander, John. 1793.
Alexander, Rev. T., Carncastle.
1806.
Alexander, Rev. Thomas. 1793.
Allan, Thomas, Islandbane. 1799.
Allen, Miss A., Lisnataylor.
1806.
Allen, Samuel, Esq. 1793.
Allen, Samuel, T:patrick. 1799.
Anderson, Drummond, Belfast.
1806.
Anderson, John, Whitehouse.
1799.
Anderson, Robert, Carmoney.
1793.
Anderson, Thomas, Rickamore.
1806.
Andrew, John, Roughfort. 1799.
Andrews, Mic., Belfast. 1806.
Annesley, William, Whitehouse.
1799.
Armstrong, John, Ballyutogue.
1806.
Armstrong, John, Belfast. 1806.
Armstrong, John, jun.,
Ballymartin. 1793.
Armstrong, Miss, Rose-park. 1806.
Armstrong, Robert, Malone. 1806.
Armstrong, Wm., Comber. 1799.
Arot, John, Ballylesson. 1806.
Arthur, Mrs., Carrickfergus. 1806.
Ashcroft, Edward, Whitehouse.
1799.

Auchinleck, William, jun., Belfast.
1799.

B

Bailie, John, jun., Roughfort.
1806.
Bailie, John, Roughfort. 1806.
Bailie, Robert, Hollywood. 1806.
Baird, William, White-house. 1806.
Ballynure Book-club, 2 copies.
1806.
Bankhead, John. 1793.
Bankhead, Miss Mary, Greenfield.
1806.
Barber, Samuel, British. 1806.
Barklie, David, Malusk. 1806.
Barklie, Mrs., Drumadarach. 1799.
Barklie, Thomas, Ballynashee.
1806.
Barnet, John, Roughfort. 1793.
Barr, Alexander, Belfast. 1799.
Barr, H. P., Belfast. 1799.
Barr, John, Templepatrick. 1799.
Barr, John, Templepatrick. 1806.
Barron, Jo., Roughfort. 1799.
Barron, Joseph, Roughfort. 1793.
Barry, Mr., Glen-Oak. 1793.
Barton, Joseph, Bareness. 1806.
Bean, John, Belfast. 1806.
Beattie, George, near Roughfort.
1793.
Beattie, Miss, Courthill. 1793.
Beattie, Thomas, Roughfort. 1806.
Beattie, Thos., Roughfort. 1799.
Beatty, Arthur, Court-hill. 1806.
Beatty, John, Ballynure. 1806.
Beatty, Thomas. Dunadry. 1793.
Beaty, Robert, Dromore. 1799.
Beck, Samuel, Belfast. 1793.
Beck, Samuel. 1806.
Beels, Robert, Malone. 1806.
Beggs, Alexander, Courthill. 1799.
Beggs, William, Ballynashee. 1806.
Beggs, William, Ballyrobin. 1806.

Begs, Alexander, Killead. 2 copies. 1793.

Bell, Francis, Carmoney. 1799.

Bell, James, Pigeontown. 1806.

Bell, Jane, Ballybought. 1806.

Bell, John, Greencastle. 1806.

Bell, Martha. 1806.

Bell, Robert, Pigeontown. 1806

Bell, Samuel, Ballyutogue. 1806.

Bell, William, Roughfort. 1793.

Bell, Wm. J., Killead. 1806.

Berry, Henry, Loughermore. 1806.

Biggar, David. 1793.

Bill, Alex., Burnside. 1806.

Birkmires, Samuel, Craigarogan. 1799.

Birkmires, Wm., Craigarogan. 1806.

Birnie, David, Claudy. 1799.

Birnie, John, Belfast. 1806.

Black, Andrew, Carmevey. 1806.

Black, Elenor, Carmevey. 1806.

Black, James, Crosshill. 1799.

Black, James, Crumlin. 1806.

Black, John Henderson, Woodford. 1793.

Black, John, student, near Portglenone. 1793.

Blacketter, John, Belfast. 1799.

Blain, George, Carnanee. 1799.

Blair, Mrs. 1793.

Blow, Alison, Dunadry. 1806.

Blow, Charlotte, Dunadry. 1806.

Blow, D. M., Dunadry. 1806.

Blow, James, Dunadry. 1793.

Blow, James, Esq., Dunadry. 1806.

Blow, James, jun., Dunadry. 1806.

Boal, Adam, Donagor. 1793.

Boal, Miss E., Rathmore. 1806.

Boomer, James, Belfast. 1793.

Boyd, David, Belfast. 1806.

Boyd, David, Killead. 1806.

Boyd, Hugh, Roughfort. 2 copies. 1799.

Boyd, James, Bareness. 1806.

Boyd, John P., Bareness. 1806.

Boyd, Margret, Killead. 1806.

Boyd, Miss J., Bareness. 1806.

Boyd, Nath., Carmoney. 1799.

Boyd, Rev. H., Rathfriland. 1806.

Boyd, William, Belfast. 1806.

Boyd, William, Rathfriland. 1806.

Boyd, William. 1793.

Boyle, John, Largey. 1799.

Bradford, Alexander, surgeon, Roughfort. 1793.

Bradford, Mrs., Roughfort. 1806.

Bradford, William, Roughfort. 1806.

Bradshaw, John. 1793.

Brady, John, Roughfort. 1806.

Breckenridge, Thomas. 1806.

Brians, Miss, Stranfield. 1806.

Brice, William, Belfast. 1806.

Briggs, Andrew. 1799.

Brigs, Robert. 1799.

Britain, James, Purdy's-burn. 1806.

Briton, Travor, Purdy's-burn. 1806.

Broadford, William, Rathfriland. 1806.

Brown, John A., Belfast. 1793.

Brown, John, Antrim. 1799.

Brown, John, Belfast. 1806.

Brown, John. 1793.

Brown, Joseph, Warringstown. 2 copies. 1806.

Brown, Samuel, Warringstown. 2 copies. 1806.

Brown, William, Roughfort. 1806.

Brown, Wm., Roughfort. 1799.

Bruce, John, jun., Antrim. 1793.

Bryants, Mrs., Crumlin. 1799.

Bryants, Mrs., Stranfield. 1806.

Brynan, John, Broad-island. 1806.

Bryson, Henry Bell. 1793.

Bryson, Rev. William, Antrim. 1793.

Burden, Daniel, Belfast. 1793.

Burleigh, Miss, Carrickfergus. 1806.

Burleigh, W. D., Esq., Carrickfergus. 1806.

Burns, Matt., Roughfort. 1806.

Burnside, Miss A., Belfast. 1806.

Burrows, Timothy, Hydepark. 1806.

Byrne, Edward. 1793.

Byrne, John, Esq., Lisburn. 1793.

C

Caddell, John, attorney,
          Rathfriland. 1806.
Cain, Sam. R., Ballyutoag. 1799.
Caldwell, George, Whitehouse.
          1799.
Caldwell, John, Maghramorne.
          1806.
Caldwell, William, Brouslee. 1793.
Callam, John, Dunmurry. 1806.
Callam, John, Malone. 1806.
Callwell, Elizabeth, Belfast. 1793.
Callwell, Robert, Belfast.
          10 copies. 1793.
Callwell, Robert, Belfast. 1799.
Calwell, James, Dublin. 1793.
Calwell, John. 1799.
Calwell, John. 1799.
Calwell, Nathaniel, Dublin.
          6 copies. 1793.
Calwell, Robert, Springfield. 1806.
Cameron, John, Lyle. 1799.
Cameron, Samuel, jun., Bareness.
          1806.
Campbel, John, Roughfort. 1793.
Campbell, Clotworthy, Crumlin.
          1806.
Campbell, Geo. S. 1806.
Campbell, Henry, Killead. 1793.
Campbell, Hugh, Carmoney.
          1799.
Campbell, James, Crumlin.
          2 copies. 1793.
Campbell, James M. N.,
          Roughfort. 1799.
Campbell, James M. N.,
          Roughfort. 1799.
Campbell, James, Rockhill. 1806.
Campbell, Jas., Crooked-stone.
          1806.
Campbell, John, Dunadry. 1793.
Campbell, John, Whitehouse.
          1799.
Campbell, Mrs., Killally. 1806.
Campbell, R., Crumlin. 1793.

Campbell, Rev. Robert,
          Templepatrick. 1799.
Campbell, Rev. Robert, A.M.,
          Templepatrick. 1806.
Campbell, Stephenson, Antrim.
          1793.
Campbell, William, Crumlin.
          1806.
Campbell, William, Tully. 1806.
Carleton, Edward, Blaris. 1806.
Carruth, Benjamin, Long-fauld.
          1806.
Carruth, Benjamin, Roughfort.
          1799.
Carruth, Benjamin, Trench. 1793.
Carson, James, Ballyhill. 1806.
Carson, Jean, Ballyutoag. 1799.
Carson, John, Drumbo. 1806.
Caruth, Loudy, Trench. 1806.
Cathcart, Hugh, Ballycarry. 1806.
Cavart, Mary, Bareness. 1806.
Cavart, Thomas, Dundrod. 1806.
Cavenagh, William, Roughfort.
          1799.
Cavenagh, William, Roughfort.
          1806.
Chambers, Brice, Belfast. 1806.
Charters, John, Antrim. 1806.
Clanny, Hugh, Broadisland. 1806.
Clark, Francis, Carmoney. 1799.
Clark, Robert, Belfast. 1806.
Clements, Andrew, Ballygomartin.
          1799.
Clements, Margre, Ligoneil. 1806.
Close, James, Ballycarry. 1806.
Coaman, James, Carmevy. 1799.
Coaman, James, Carmevy. 1806.
Coaman, Samuel, Carmevy. 1806.
Coburn, George. 1793.
Cochran, Geo., Belfast. 1806.
Colbreath, John, Malone. 1806.
Colvin, Mary. 1806.
Conning, Patrick, Carnlea. 1793.
Cooper, James, Muckamore. 1806.
Cooper, James, near Muckamore.
          1793.
Coperthwaite, Ben., Carmoney.
          1799.
Corry, Robert, Ballyutoag. 1799.

Corry, Robert, Ligoneil. 1806.
Couples, Rev. Snowden. 1793.
Courtney, Eliza, Claughanduff.
    1806.
Courtney, Hannah, Claughanduff.
    1806.
Courtney, James, Claughanduff.
    1793.
Courtney, James, Claughanduff.
    1806.
Courtney, Jas., Doagh. 2 copies.
    1806.
Courtney, Jas. jun., Claughenduff.
    1799.
Courtney, John, Templepatrick.
    1793.
Cowan, James, Rathfriland. 1806.
Cowan, Robert. Roughfort. 1793.
Cowie, John, Ballyhanwood. 1806.
Craft, John, Redhill. 1806.
Craig, John, Belfast. 1799.
Craig, John, Dunmurry. 1806.
Craig, John, near Roughfort.
    1793.
Craig, John, Roughfort. 1799.
Craig, Mr., Killead. 1793.
Cranmer, Mr., White house. 1806.
Crawford, Matthew, Balloo. 1806.
Crawford, Miss, Killead. 1806.
Crawford, Sam., Belfast. 1799.
Crossley, John, Lisburn. 1806.
Crozier, James, Belfast. 1806.
Crymble, Charles, Esq. 1793.
Crymble, Miss. 1793.
Culloden, Pat., Carmoney. 1799.
Cunningham, Adam. 1793.
Cunningham, Andrew. 1793.
Cunningham, Crooked-stone.
    1806.
Cunningham, John. 1793.
Curell, John, Drumana. 1806.

D

Dalrymple, James, Lowtown. 1799.
Dalrymple, John, Roughfort. 1793.
Dalrymple, Sam., Roughfort. 1799.

Dalrymple, Samuel, Roughfort.
    1806.
Darley, Arthur. 1793.
Davey, Samuel. 1799.
Davies, William, Belfast. 1799.
Davis, Francis, Belfast. 1799.
Davison, James, Antrim. 1793.
Davison, Mr., Crumlin-bridge.
    1793.
Dawson, Thomas, Ballymather.
    1806.
Dempsey, Patrick, Killead. 1793.
Dickey, John, Crumlin. 1793.
Dickson, A., Muckomore. 1806.
Dickson, Mrs., Carmoney. 1799.
Dickson, Richard, Bog-house.
    1806.
Doagh 2nd Book-club. 1793.
Doah Book-club. 1793.
Dobbs, Rev. Robert. 1793.
Doherty and Simms, Belfast. 1799.
Doherty, Hugh, Whitehouse.1799.
Dollars, Thomas, Ballynure. 1806.
Donaldson, Wm., Drum-bridge.
    1806.
Donnell, James, Antrim. 1793.
Donnelly, Hugh, White-house.
    1806.
Dormant, John. 1799.
Douglas, A., Lieut., Randalstown.
    2 copies. 1806.
Douglas, Paul, Parkgate. 1793.
Dunlop, Alex., Boghead. 1806.
Dunlop, James, Belfast. 1806.
Dunlop, John, Malone. 1806.

E

Eaken, Dan., Milltown. 1806.
Edenlees, Wm., Esq., General Post
    Office, Dublin. 2 copies.
    1806.
Edwards, Benjamin, Belfast. 1799.
Erskine, William, Seacash. 1806.
Evins, Robert, Rock. 1806.

F

Farrel, William, Roughfort. 1806.

Farrell, William, Roughfort. 1799.
Fee, John, Roughfort. 1799.
Ferguson, Hugh, Hyde-park. 1806.
Ferguson, John, Malone. 1806.
Ferguson, Mrs., Hydepark. 1799.
Ferguson, Thomas, Hyde park. 1806.
Ferguson, Thomas, jun., Hyde park. 1806.
Ferguson, Thomas, Lower Holestone. 1799.
Ferguson, Thos., Hyde-park. 1799.
Ferguson, William, Belfast. 1799.
Fergusson, Andrew, Knockin. 1793.
Fergusson, Francis, Dunagore. 1793.
Fergusson, John, Muckamore. 1793.
Fergusson, John. 1793.
Fergusson, Thomas, Four-Mile Burn. 1799.
Fergusson, William, near Derry. 1793.
Ferris, Thomas, Belfast. 1799.
Finlay, David, Hillsborough. 1806.
Finlay, jun., Ballymartin. 1806.
Finlay, Mr., jun. 1793.
Finlay, Samuel, Woodburn. 1793.
Finlay, William, Ballymartin. 1793.
Finlay, Wm., Ballymartin. 1799.
Finlay, Wm., jun., Carrickfergus. 1806.
Finlay, Wm., student, Carrickfergus. 2 copies. 1806.
Forbes, Doctor John, Carnlea. 1793.
Forbis, William, Antrim. 1793.
Forsythe, George. 2 copies. 1806.
Fry, Hugh, Ballymartin. 1806.

G

Galt, Ann, Rickamore. 1806.
Galt, James, Belfast. 1793.
Garland, Alex., Carmevey. 1806.
Gelston, Thomas. 1793.

George, John, Killead. 1806.
Gibson, Andrew, Gibsonstown. 1799.
Gibson, James, Belfast. 1799.
Gibson, James, Belfast. 1806.
Gibson, John K., Gibson's town. 1806.
Gibson, Miss, Belfast. 1806.
Gibson, Rev. J., Cross-hill. 1793.
Gibson, William, schoolmaster, Doagh. 1793.
Giffin, Sam. B., Boghouse. 1806.
Gihon, Andw., jun., Ballymena. 1806.
Gihon, Mr., Ballymena. 1793.
Gihon, Robert. 1793.
Gilbert, William, Dublin. 6 copies. 1793.
Gillis, Jane, Kilcross. 1806.
Given, James, Largey. 1806.
Gordon, John, jun., Loughermore. 1806.
Gordon, Mr., Loughermore. 1806.
Gordon, William. 1793.
Gourley, Alex., Bareness. 1806.
Gowdie, Chas. O. N., C.odore. 1806.
Graham, Hugh. 1799.
Graham, John, Belfast. 1793.
Graham, John, Whitepark. 1799.
Graham, John. 1793.
Graham, Stewart, Belfast. 1799.
Graham, Timothy, Carmoney. 1799.
Grant, James, Belfast. 1793.
Green, Alexer., T:patrick. 1799.
Green, William, Whitehouse. 1799.
Greenfield, James. 1806.
Greenfield, Robert, Belfast. 1799.
Greer, Samuel. 1806.
Grey, M., Belfast. 1806.
Grimshaw, C. M., Whitehouse. 1806.
Grimshaw, Edmd., Whitehouse. 1806.
Grimshaw, J., Whitehouse. 1799.
Grimshaw, James, Whitehouse. 1806.

Grimshaw, N., jun., Whitehouse.
1799.
Grimshaw, R., Whitehouse. 1806.
Grogan, James, Belfast. 1793.
Grogan, Robert. 1793.
Gunning, Miss. 1793.

H

Hamil, James, Belfast. 1799.
Hamilton, Adam, Roughfort.
1793.
Hamilton, John, Roughfort. 1799.
Hamilton, Mr., Malusk. 1806.
Hanna, Robert, Cottenmount.
1806.
Hannah, James, Crumlin. 1806.
Hannah, Wm., Ballynadrentah.
1806.
Hanon, James, Leacash. 1799.
Harper, Hugh, Belfast. 1793.
Harper, Rev. Jas., Clady. 1806.
Harper, Thomas, Belfast. 1799.
Harper, William, Belfast. 1806.
Harper, William, near
Templepatrick. 1793.
Hartley, George, Belfast. 1806.
Hay, Francis, Belfast. 1793.
Hay, Sam., Ballyeaston. 1806.
Hays, Samuel, Whitehouse. 1799.
Hazlett, John. 1793.
Henderson, George, Belfast. 1799.
Henderson, J. 1793.
Henderson, John, Ballymacaret.
1806.
Henderson, Robert, Killead. 1806.
Henderson, William, Belfast. 1799.
Henderson, William. 1793.
Henning, John, student, Killead.
1806.
Henning, Miss, Killead. 1806.
Herbinson, James, Dunagore.
1806.
Hetherington, Hugh, Skilginaban.
1806.
Hill, David, Ballynure. 1806.
Hodgson, Robert, Belfast. 1799.
Hodgson, Robert, Belfast. 1793.
Hogg, William, Belfast. 1799.

Hollywood, John, Hollymount.
1806.
Holmes, James, jun., near
Templepatrick. 1793.
Holmes, John, T:patrick. 1799.
Holmes, Thomas, Islandmagee.
1806.
Holywood, Alex., Malone. 1799.
Hood, James, Belfast. 1793.
Hope, James, Craigarogan. 1806.
Hope, Luke Mullan, Craigarogan.
1806.
Hopes, John, Belfast. 1799.
Hopps, John, Belfast. 1799.
Horner, Hugh, Whitehouse. 1806.
Horner, Thomas, Roughfort.
1799.
Horner, Thomas, Roughfort.
1806.
Horseman, Margaret,
Templepatrick. 1793.
Horseman, Miss M., Tobergill.
1799.
Howe, Mrs., Greencastle. 1806.
Hughes, John, bookseller, Belfast.
25 copies. 1793.
Hughes, Thomas, Belfast. 1806.
Hull, Miss, Carrickfergus. 1806.
Hull, Mr., Belfast. 1793.
Hull, William, Belfast. 1799.
Hunter, Miss S., Boulticonnel.
1806.
Hunter, William, Antrim. 1799.
Hunter, William, Belfast. 1799.
Hunter, William, Crumlin. 1806.
Hunter, Wm., Esq., Dunmurry.
1806.
Huston, John, Ballyeaston. 1806.
Huston, John, Hyde-park. 1806.
Huston, Thos., Islandreagh. 1799.
Hutchinson, John, Antrim. 1806.
Hyndman, James, Belfast. 1793.
Hyndman, Robert, Belfast. 1793.

I

Inglis, Daniel, Roughfort. 1799.
Inglis, John, Roughfort. 1806.
Inglis, Richard, Roughfort. 1806.
Irwin, James, New-bridge. 1806.

J

Jackson, William. 1793.
James, John, Roughfort. 1799.
Jameson, Miss E. M., Killead. 1806.
Jameson, Robert, Muckamore. 1799.
Jameson, Thos., Dunagore. 1806.
Jamison, Thomas, B. Bareness. 1799.
Jamison, Thos., Ballysavage. 1799.
Jelly, Alex., jun., Lisburn. 1806.
Jelly, Robert, Lisburn. 2 copies. 1806.
Johnson, John, Killead. 1806.
Johnson, Mary, Rickamore. 1793.
Johnson, Miss, Glenavy. 1806.
Johnson, Miss, Islandbawn. 1793.
Johnson, Miss, Islandbawn. 1799.
Johnson, Sam., Ballypallady. 1799.
Johnson, Thomas, Malone. 1806.
Johnson, William, Belfast. 1799.
Johnston, Jane, Miss, Burnside. 1806.
Johnston, Jas., Dunagore. 1806.
Johnston, Robert, Belfast. 1806.
Jones, Wm., Belfast. 1806.

K

Kean, Thomas, Belfast. 1793.
Kelly, James, Loughermore. 1806.
Kelly, William. 1806.
Kelso, Andrew, Whitehouse. 1799.
Kelso, Edward, Roughfort. 1806.
Kelso, Ephm., Craigarogan. 1806.
Kelso, G., Roughfort. 1806.
Kelso, Henry, Roughfort. 1793.
Kelso, Henry, Roughfort. 1806.
Kelso, James, B. Bareness. 1799.
Kelso, Jas., jun., Craigarogan. 1806.
Kelso, Wm., Roughfort. 1806.
Kelso, Wm., Windy-hill. 1806.
Kemp, Robert, Lurgan. 1793.
Kennedy, A., Belfast. 1793.
Kennedy, Alexander, Belfast. 1793.
Kennedy, Charles, Lisburn. 1793.

Kennedy, J., Miss, Drumaul. 1806.
Kent, Wm., Belfast. 1806.
Kiernan, James, Belfast. 1793.
Killead Literary Society. 1806.
Kilpatrick, Alex., Antrim. 1806.
Kilpatrick, Thomas, Corbilly. 1806.
Kirk, James, White-house. 1806.
Kirk, Mr. 1793.
Kirk, Mrs., Carrickfergus. 1806.
Kirker, G., Carnaghlis. 1806.
Kirkpatrick, Dan., Roughfort. 1806.
Kirkpatrick, Daniel, Roughfort. 1793.
Kirkwood, Hugh, Ballyeaston. 1806.
Kirkwood, Robert, White-house. 1806.
Knox, George, Belfast. 1793.

L

Lamb, James, Belfast. 1793.
Lamont, Aeneas, Belfast. 1793.
Lanauze, George, Belfast. 1806.
Lappan, George, Antrim. 1799.
Lawther, John, jun., Tobergill. 1806.
Ledlie, Alexander, Antrim. 2 copies. 1793.
Lee, John. 1793.
Legg, Miss, Belfast. 1793.
Legg, Mrs. 1793.
Leonard, Peter, Hillsborough. 1799.
Lepper, Max., White-Abbey. 1793.
Lewis, Edward, Muckamore. 1793.
Lewis, John, Ballyrobbin. 2 copies 1806.
Liddie, M. E., Malone. 1806.
Logan, James, Seacash. 1806.
Loggan, James, Sea-cash. 1793.
Loughridge, William, Captain, near Ballymena, 6 copies. 1793.
Love, Richard. 1806
Lowry, J., Miss, Malone. 1806.
Luke, Samuel, Belfast. 1799.

Luke, Samuel. 1806.
Lyle, John, Belfast. 1793.
Lyle, John, Muckamore. 1799.
Lyle, John. 1806.
Lyle, Thomas, jun., Belfast. 1799.
Lyster, John, Dunmurry. 1806.

M

M'Adam, George, Belfast. 1799.
M'Adam, John, Ballyrobert. 1799.
M'Adam, John, Belfast. 1806.
M'Adam, Mrs., Belfast. 1806.
M'Adam, Robert, Belfast. 1806.
M'Adam, Sam., T:patrick. 1799.
M'Adam, William, Ligoniel. 1806.
M'Adam, Wm., Belfast. 1806.
M'Alister, Charles, Belfast. 1806.
M'Alister, James, Craigarogan.
        1806.
M'Alpin, John, Belfast. 1806.
M'Auley, Mr., Gab. 1806.
M'Auley, Rev. Andw., Rathfryland.
        1806.
M'Avoy, John, Rathfryland. 1806.
M'Bride, Alex., Shanogueston.
        2 copies.
M'Bride, Thomas, Muckamore.
        1793.
M'Bride, William, Muckamore.
        1799.
M'Bride, William, Muckamore.
        1793.
M'Bryde, Francis, Boughill. 1806.
M'Bryde, John. 1806.
M'Bryde, Nath., Balynalough.
        1806.
M'Caskill, W., Colonel, I. F.
        Officer, Belfast. 1806.
M'Clean, Adam, Belfast. 1799.
M'Clean, Andrew, Belfast. 1793.
M'Clean, Andrew, Esq. 1806.
M'Clean, John, Lieut., 91st.
        Regiment, Dublin.
        2 copies. 1806.

M'Clean, Arch., Lieut.,

        28th. British Militia,
        Musselborough.
        2 copies. 1806.
M'Clean, Robert, Whitehouse.
        1806.
M'Clinton, A., Whitehouse. 1799.
M'Clinton, A., Whitehouse. 1806.
M'Clinton, John, Hyde-park. 1806.
M'Clinton, Robert, White-house.
        1806.
M'Clughan, J.B., Bareness. 1806.
M'Cluney, Robert, Belfast. 1799.
M'Clurg, James, Claghanduff.
        1806.
M'Clurken, George, Belfast. 1806.
M'Comb, Alex., Islandmagee.
        1806.
M'Comb, Samuel, Belfast. 1793.
M'Comb, Samuel, Belfast. 1799.
M'Comb, Thomas, Carmevey.
        1806.
M'Cormick, Agnes, Malone. 1806.
M'Cormick, James, Belfast. 1793.
M'Cormick, James, Belfast. 1793.
M'Cormick, Miss A., Roughfort.
        1799.
M'Coughtry, Robert. 1799.
M'Cracken, Henry J. 1793.
M'Cullen, William, Antrim. 1799.
M'Curdy, Alex., Belfast. 1806.
M'Dermott, Edward, Crumlin.
        1806.
M'Donald, James, Carmoney.
        1799.
M'Donald, Surgeon, Crumlin.
        1806.

M'Dougall, A., Esq., Logan.
        5 copies. 1806.
M'Dougall, Alex., Capt.,
        72nd. Regiment,
        Dunolly, Castlehern,
        North Britain.
        2 copies. 1806.
M'Dougall, Alex., Lieut.,
        53rd. Regiment,
        Madras.
        5 copies.1806.

M'Dougall, Alex., Major, Crescent, Castlebellingham, lately. 1806.

M'Dougall, D., Capt., 28th. B. Regt., Edinburgh. 5 copies. 1806.

M'Dougall, John, Esq., Admiral of the Blue, Plymouth. 4 copies. 1806.

M'Dougall, John, Mr., 44th. Regiment, Malta. 2 copies. 1806.

M'Dougall, Mrs. 6 copies. 1806.

M'Dougall, Patrick, Esq., of Gallanuch & Hayfield, Argyleshire. 5 copies. 1806.

M'Dougall, Thomas, Whitehouse. 1799.

M'Dougall, Thomas, Whitehouse. 1806.

M'Dougall, W. B., Esq., 44th. Regiment, Malta. 1806.

M'Dougall, Wm. B., Castle Upton. 5 copies. 1806.

M'Dowel, Alexander, Antrim. 1793.

M'Dowell, Arch., Dunmurry. 1806.

M'Ervil, Mr., Kilmakevit. 1793.

M'Ewen, James, Roughfort. 1806.

M'Faddin, Eliza, Kilcross. 1806.

M'Fee, Archibald, Whitehouse. 1799.

M'Fee, Daniel, Whitehouse. 1799.

M'Fode, Wm., Dunagore. 1806.

M'Gaghey, Robert, Belfast. 1806.

M'Garagh, John, Belfast. 1793.

M'Garret, William, Belfast. 1806.

M'Gaw, Joseph, Ballivezie. 1793.

M'Gaw, Wm., Toberagnew. 1806.

M'Giffen, William. 1799.

M'Giveren, John, White-house. 1806.

M'Glathry, John, Belfast. 1799.

M'Golpin, Mrs. 1793.

M'Gowan, R. 1793.

M'Gowan, Robert, Carrickfergus. 1799.

M'Gowan, Robert, Londonderry. 1793.

M'Gowen, James, Marshalstown. 1799.

M'Ilmeen, George. 1793.

M'Ilwain, John, Artist, T:patrick. 1799.

M'Ilwain, John, Claghanduff. 1806.

M'Ilwain, John, Rathfryland. 1806.

M'Intyre, G. 1806.

M'Keag, Miss, Lisnataylor. 1806.

M'Keage, John, Dunagore. 1793.

M'Kean, John, Belfast. 1806.

M'Keen, James, Carnanee. 1806.

M'Keever, John, Ballycastle. 1793.

M'Kelvey, Andrew, Roughfort. 1806.

M'Kelvy, Alex. B., Roughfort. 1799.

M'Kelvy, Alex., Roughfort. 1799.

M'Kelvy, John, Malusk. 1799.

M'Key, John, Loughermore. 1806.

M'Kibbin, James, Belfast. 1793.

M'Kinley, John, Ballycarry. 1806.

M'Larnin, Henry, Balymather. 1806.

M'Larnin, James, Malone. 1806.

M'Main, Samuel, Belfast. 1799.

M'Master, Miss, Killead. 1806.

M'Master, Mr., Crumlin Mills. 1793.

M'Millan, Agnes, Trench. 1793.

M'Millan, John, Ballymena. 25 copies. 1806.

M'Mullan, James, Malusk. 1806.

M'Mullan, Wm., White-house. 1806.

M'Murray, Jesse, Belfast. 1793.

M'Naghton, Samuel, Belfast. 1793.

M'Neilly, James, Carngranny. 1793.

M'Neilly, John, Carngranny. 1799.

M'Neilly, John, jun., Carngranny. 1793.

M'Neilly, John, Trench. 1799.

M'Neilly, Margaret, sen.,
    Carngranny. 1793.
M'Neilly, Mrs. S., Carngranny.
    1799.
M'Pherson, James, Belfast. 1793.
M'Pherson, Thomas, Todmount.
    1806.
M'Shane, P., Crumlin. 1793.
M'Stocher, Jas., Carnmoney. 1806.
M'Teer, James, Doagh. 1806.
M'Vickar, James Esq.,
    Templepatrick. 1793.
M'William, Mrs., Banbridge. 1799.
M'William, Mrs., Banbridge. 1806.
Macartney, John, Belfast. 1799.
Mackey, Alexander, Greenmount.
    1799.
Maclave, Geo., Summerhill. 1799.
Macomb, David, Carnmoney.
    1806.
Madden, John, Templepatrick
    Infantry. 1799.
Madden, John. 1806.
Magee, Henry, Dundroad. 1806.
Magee, John, Dundroad. 1806.
Magee, Nathaniel, Newbridge.
    1793.
Magee, William, Belfast. 10 copies.
    1793.
Magee, Wm., Belfast. 1799.
Magill, Geo., Malone.
Magill, Hugh, Belfast. 1799.
Maitain, S., Miss, Malone. 1806.
Malcom, Samuel, Belfast. 1793.
Malone, William, Whitehouse.
    1793.
Malone, Wm., Whitehouse. 1799.
Marshal, John, Roughfort. 1799.
Marshall, James, Carmoney. 1793.
Marshall, Sam., Hill-hall. 1806.
Martin, George, Belfast. 1793.
Martin, John, Dunadry. 1806.
Martin, Samuel, Antrim. 1799.
Mawhinny, John, Lyle. 1806.
Mayne, John. 1806.
Meighan, Arthur, Muckamore.
    1793.
Mercer, Arthur. 1806.
Milford, Mr., Cross-hill. 1793.

Miller, Alex., Ballynure. 1806.
Miller, John, Belfast. 1806.
Milliken, Thos., Ballytweedy. 1806.

Milliken, William, Carmoney.
    1799.
Miniss, Mrs., Islandban. 1806.
Miniss, Robert, Woodville. 1806.
Moat, Isaiah, Roughfort. 1806.
Moat, Sam., Lyle. 1806.
Molyneux, Margaret, British. 1806.
Montgomery, A., Belfast. 1806.
Montgomery, H., student, Killead.
    2 copies. 1806.
Montgomery, Hugh, Rock. 1806.
Montgomery, Joseph. 1806.
Montgomery, Miss, Brookville.
    1806.
Montgomery, Mrs., Boulticonnel.
    1806.
Montgomery, Robert, Balyeaston.
    1806.
Montgomery, Robert. 1793.
Montgomery, Thomas,
    Ballymarlough. 1793.
Moore, Ann. 1793.
Moore, Arthur, Crooked-stone.
    1806.
Moore, John, Claudy. 1799.
Moore, John, Dungonnel. 1806.
Moore, John, jun., Killead. 1793.
Moore, S. J. Miss, British. 1806.
Moore, Thomas, Carnanee. 1799.
Moore, William, British. 1806.
Moorhead, H. W., Lisnataylor.
    1806.
Morrison, Jane, Crooked-stone.
    1806.
Morrison, John, Crooked-stone.
    1806.
Morrison, William. 1793.
Morrow, James, Carmoney. 1799.
Mossman, Samuel, Kilcross. 1806.
Mullan, James, Whitehouse. 1799.
Mullan, Luke, Roughfort. 1793.
Mullinex, John, Dungonel. 1799.
Murdoch, James, Trench. 1799.
Murdoch, Mary, Mrs., Belfast.
    1806.

Murdoch, Richard, Belfast. 1799.
Murdoch, Samuel, Malusk. 1806.
Murdock, David, Craigarogan.
    1806.
Murdock, John, Skilginaban. 1806.
Murdock, Mrs., Roughfort. 1806.
Murphy, Miss, Islandmagee. 1806.
Murray, Dalway, Carmoney. 1799.
Murray, F. H., Kilultagh. 1799.
Murray, Hugh, Purdy's-burn. 1806.

N

Neeson, W., Crumlin. 1793.
Neil, Miss, Templepatrick. 1793.
Neil, Thomas, Boston in America.
    12 copies. 1793.
Neill, Robert. 1806.
Neilson, Samuel, Belfast. 1793.
Nesbit, John, Claughenduff. 1806.
Nevill, Joseph, Lambeg. 1793.
Nickle, David, Belfast. 1806.
Nixon, Jacob, Belfast. 1793.
Nowlan, Thomas. 1793.
Nugent, Captain, 38th. Regiment.
    1793.

O

O'Brien, Louisa. 1793.
O'Farrel, John, White-house. 1806.
O'Hara, Henry, Dunadry. 1806.
O'Neil, Daniel, Muckamore. 1799.
O'Neill, Daniel, Antrim. 1793.
Oakman, Mary, Miss, Belfast. 1806.
Oakman, William, Belfast. 1793.
Officer, Robert, Ballyhill. 1806.
Oliphant, Wm., Roughfort. 1806.
Orr, Alex., Belfast. 1806.
Orr, Andrew, Whitehouse. 1799.
Orr, James, Ballycarry. 1806.
Orr, James, jun., Ballycarry. 1793.
Orr, John, Carnmoney. 1806.
Orr, Rev. Mr., Killead. 1793.
Orr, Rev. Mr., Killead. 1806.
Osborne, John C., Belfast. 1806.
Owens, Wm. G., Taldarg. 1799.
Owens, Wm., Holestone. 1799.

P

Park, James, Ballynure. 1806.
Park, Jane. 1793.

Park, John, Ballynure. 1806.
Parker, John, Carnance. 1799.
Parkinson, Thomas, Belfast. 1793.
Patterson, James, Ballyrobert.
    1799.
Patterson, James, Belfast. 1793.
Patterson, James, Roughfort. 1793.
Patterson, John, Roughfort. 1799.
Patterson, John, Roughfort. 1793.
Patterson, John, Roughfort. 1806.
Patterson, Miss, Belfast. 1806.
Pattison, Thos., Wilmount. 1806.
Pattison, William, Wilmount. 1806.
Patton, Mark, Belfast. 1799.
Patton, Wm., Ballyeaston. 1806.
Paul, Rev. Mr. 6 copies. 1806.
Penny, Wm., Carrickfergus. 1806.
Philips, Wm., Ballynure. 1806.
Phillips, James. 1793.
Pinkertoe, Wm., Roughfort. 1806.
Pinkerton, James, Belfast. 1793.
Pinkerton, James, Greencastle.
    1806.
Potts, Thomas, Belfast. 1799.
Potts, Thomas, Belfast. 1793.
Price, Rev. J., Killead. 1793.
Procter, William, Belfast. 1799.
Purdy, Mary. 1799.

Q

Quin, Wm., White-house. 1806.
Quinn, Arthur, Belfast. 1799.

R

Rabb, John, Belfast. 1793.
Radcliff, William, Belfast. 1799.
Rainey, Hugh, Crossnacreevy.
    1806.
Rainey, John, Falls. 1806.
Ray, James, Ballycarry. 1806.
Rea, Dan., jun., Ballinaglough.
    1799.
Rea, Daniel, Ballynaglough. 1806.

Rea, John, Killmakee. 1799.
Rea, Robert. 1799.
Rea, Samuel, jun., Lisle. 1793.
Reford, Joseph, Templepatrick. 1793.
Reid, J., jun., Waterside. 2 copies. 1806.
Reid, James, Belfast. 1806.
Reid, Paul, Roughfort. 1806.
Reid, Thomas, Belfast. 1799.
Reside, John, near Randalstown. 1793.
Rice, John, Belfast. 1806.
Rice, William, Malone. 1806.
Richardson, James, Belfast. 1799.
Richmond, Wm., Braid. 1806.
Riddle, John, Belfast. 1806.
Robb, Alex., jun., Carmevey. 1806.
Robb, Alex., sen., Carmevey. 1806.
Robb, John, jun., Carmevey. 1806.
Robb, Patt, Belfast. 1793.
Robb, Samuel, Lisle. 1793.
Robinson, Daniel, Belfast. 1806.
Robinson, John, Hillsborough 1793.
Robinson, Randal. 1806.
Robinson, William, near Antrim. 1793.
Robinson, Wm., Ballyutoag. 1799.
Robison, Wm., Muckamore. 1799.
Rogers, John. 1806.
Roney, Alex., Danturky. 1806.
Ross, Robert, Belfast. 1806.
Ross, Sam., Bareness. 2 copies. 1806.

Ruddock, Margaret, Carmoney. 1799.
Rusk, John, Summerhill. 1799.
Russel, Samuel, Roughfort. 1799.
Russell, Joseph, Rosepark. 1806.
Russell, Samuel, Belfast. 1793.

S

Sanderson, James, Doagh. 1793.
Sanderson, Miss, Kilead. 1806.
Sargineer, Mr., Belfast. 1793.
Sayers, John, Belfast. 1799.

Scott, James, Belfast. 1806.
Scott, James, medical student, Edinburgh. 1793.
Scott, John, Belfast. 1793.
Scott, John, Skilginaban. 1806.
Scott, Robert. Belfast. 1793.
Scott, Samuel, Hyde-park. 1806.
Scott, William, Ballyrobin. 1793.
Scott, William, Lyle. 1799.
Scott, William, near Dunadry. 1793.
Scrymgeour, John, Belfast. 1799.
Service, John. 1806.
Service, Robert, Dunamoy. 1806.
Shanaghan, Daniel, Belfast. 1799.
Shanahan, Daniel, Belfast. 1793.
Shaw, John, Dunadry. 1806.
Shaw, William. 1793.
Shean, Robert, New-bridge. 1806.
Simm, James, Lyle. 1799.
Simm, Matt., Gibsonstown. 1799.
Simms, John, Holiwood. 1799.
Simms, William, Belfast. 1793.
Simonton, James, Belfast. 1806.
Simpson, James, Oldforge. 1806.
Simpson, John, Ballynure. 1806.
Simpson, Wm., Balymather. 1806.
Sinclaire, Rev. Mr., Newtown-Ards. 1793.
Sinclaire, Thomas, Esq. 1793.
Sloan, Oliver, Belfast. 1793.
Sloane, John, Belfast. 1799.
Smith, James, Carmoney. 1799.
Smith, James, Roughfort. 1806.
Smith, John, Carmoney. 1799.
Smith, William, Summerhill. 1799.
Smyth & Lyons, printers. 2 copies. 1806.
Smyth, J., Belfast. 1799.
Speer, Henry M., Belfast. 1793.
Speers, Eliz. A., Portglenone. 1799.
Spence, David, Belfast. 1793.
Spence, Matt., Belfast. 1806.
Spotswood, Maurice, Belfast. 1793.
Sreel, Mathew, Belfast. 1799.
Steel, Alex., Claughenduff. 1806.
Steen, James, Boghead. 1799.
Steen, James, Esq., Clady. 1806.
Steen, Mr., Antrim, 2 copies. 1793.

Sterling, James, Whitehouse. 1799.
Stevenson, George, Loughmorne.
      1806.
Stevenson, James, Belfast. 1799.
Stewart, Jas., Ballyskyagh. 1806.
Stewart, John, Belfast. 1806.
Stewart, Robert, Shankhill. 1806.
Stewart, St. John, Dunmurry. 1806.
Stewart, Thomas, Oldforge. 1806.
Stewart, Wm., Ballyearl. 1799.
Stewart, Wm., Kilead. 1806.
Stewart, Wm., Oldforge. 1806.
Stinton, Aaron, Carmoney. 1799.
Storey, James, bookseller. 1806.
Storey, Thomas, Belfast. 1793.
Stormont, James, Ligoniel. 1806.
Strichon, Adam, Antrim. 1793.
Stuart, Robert. 1793.
Sturgeon, Rev. J., A.M.,
      Ballinahinch. 1806.
Swan, Hugh, Islandreagh. 1806.
Swan, Hugh. 1793.
Swan, James, Belfast. 1799.
Swan, James. 1793.
Swan, Miss, Islandreagh. 1806.
Swan, Robert, Captain. 1793.
Swan, Wm., Rathfryland. 1806.
Swan, Wm., Rathfryland. 1806.

T

Taggart, Alexander, Belfast. 1799.
Taggart, Francis, jun., Belfast.
      1793.
Taylor, George, Malone. 1806.
Taylor, Hugh, Belfast. 1793.
Taylor, William, Belfast. 1799.
Teeling, Bartholemew, Lambeg.
      1793.
Telfair, Robert, jun., Belfast. 1806.
Templeton, William Magee,
      Belfast. 1793.
Tennent, Wm., jun., Belfast. 1806.
Thoburn, David, Malusk. 1793.
Thoburn, James, Roughfort. 1806.
Thoburn, John, Malusk. 1806.
Thoburn, John, Roughfort. 1806.
Thompson, Andw., Muckomore.
      1806.

Thompson, George. 1806.
Thompson, John, Claughenduff.
      1799.
Thompson, John, Muckamore.
      1799.
Thompson, Martha. 1806.
Thompson, Samuel, Esq.,
      Muckamore.
      20 copies. 1806.
Thompson, William, Belfast. 1799.
Thompson, William, Belfast. 1793.
Thompson, William,
      Carrickfergus. 1799.
Thomson, Andrew, Claughanduff.
      1806.
Thomson, Andrew, Claughenduff.
      1799.
Thomson, Andrew, Lysle. 1793.
Thomson, Andw., Killcross.
      1806.
Thomson, Arthur, Belfast. 1806.
Thomson, Henry, Belfast. 1806.
Thomson, J., jun., Ballymather.
      1806.
Thomson, James M'Neilly. 1793.
Thomson, John, Belfast. 1793.
Thomson, John, Claughanduff.
      1806.
Thomson, John, Lysle. 1793.
Thomson, John, Rock. 1806.
Thomson, Miss. Carmoney. 1793.
Thomson, Rev. Rob., Larne.
      1799.

Thomson, Robert, Loughermore.
      1806.
Thomson, Sam., Ballysculty. 1806.
Thomson, Sarah. 1806.
Tisdale, John, Belfast. 2 copies.
      1793.
Todd, Andrew, Toddstown. 1793.
Todd, John, Toddstown. 1793.
Trail, John, Belfast. 1806.
Trail, Robert. 1799.
Trail, Robert. 1806.
Trench, Colonel, 38th. Regiment.
      1793.

U

Upton, Colonel, Duke of York's
    Regiment, London.
    1806.

V

Vance, Rev. Mr., Belfast. 1793.

W

Walker, Samuel, Roughfort. 1799.
Walker, Wm., Roughfort. 1806.
Walkinshaw, Sam., Crumlin. 1806.
Wallace, James, Belfast. 1799.
Wallace, James, Muckamore. 1799.
Wallace, William, Lyle. 1799.
Ward, James, Belfast. 1806.
Ward, James, Lisburn. 1799.
Ward, John, Belfast. 1799.
Ward, John, Belfast. 1793.
Ward, John, Belfast. 1806.
Warrin, Hugh, bookseller, Belfast.
    1793.
Waters, Wm., Ligoneil. 1806.
Watters, James, Dunagore. 1793.
Watters, Robert, Loughermore.
    1806.
Watts, Francis, Ballypallady. 1799.
Watts, James, T:patrick. 1799.
Weir, George. 1793.
White, David, student, Glena Vale.
    1806.
White, John, Crumlin. 1806.
White, Matthew, Ballyeaston. 1806.
White, Nath., Lisnataylor. 1806.
Whiteford, John, Ballyboley. 1806.
Whiteford, John, Belfast. 1806.
Whiteford, Wm. 1806.
Wier, Samuel, Malone. 1806.
Wightman, James, Lisburn. 1799.
Wiley, Samuel, student, Craigs.
    1793.
Williamson, George, Trench. 1793.
Williamson, John, jun.,
    Carngranny. 1799.
Williamson, John, jun.,
    Carngranny. 1793.

Williamson, John, Lyle. 1806.
Williamson, John, Trench. 1799.
Williamson, Joseph, Trench. 1799.
Williamson, Joseph, Trench. 1793.
Willy, John, Dunmurry. 1806.
Wilson, Alex., Belfast. 1806.
Wilson, Clark, Belfast. 1799.
Wilson, James, Roughfort. 1806.
Wilson, John, Belfast. 1793.
Wilson, William, Whitehouse.
    1799.
Wirling, John, Belfast. 1793.
Wiseman, William. 1799.
Woods, John, Roughfort. 1806.
Wright, James, Antrim. 1793.
Wright, Joseph, Esq., attorney.
    1793.
Wright, Rev. John, Dunagore.
    1799.

Y

Young, Andrew, jun., Antrim.
    1793.
Young, James, jun., Claudy. 1799.
Young, James, jun., Lysle's hill.
    1793.
Young, James, sen., Lyle. 1799.
Young, James. 1806.
Young, Jo., B. Bareness. 1799.
Young, John, Antrim. 1793.
Young, Joseph, Bareness. 1806.
Young, Joseph, Lysle's hill. 1793.
Young, Joseph, White-house. 1806.
Young, Robert, Antrim. 1806.
Young, Robert, Bareness. 1806.
Young, Robert, jun., Antrim.
Young, Thos., Islandreagh. 1806.

TO A HEDGE - HOG

Unguarded beauty is disgrace.
                              BROOME

WHILE youthful poets, thro' the grove,
Chaunt saft their canny lays o' love,
And a' their skill exert to move
                    The darling object;
I chuse, as ye may shortly prove,
                    A rougher subject.

What fairs to bother us in sonnet,
'Bout chin an' cheek, an' brow an' bonnet?
Just chirlin like a widow'd linnet,
                    Thro' bushes lurchin;
Love's stangs are ill to thole, I own it,
                    But to my hurchin.

Thou grimest far o' grusome tykes,
Grubbing thy food by thorny dykes,
Gudefaith *thou* disna want for *pikes*,
                    Baith sharp an' rauckle;
Thou looks (L—d save's) array'd in spikes,
                    A creepin heckle!

Some say thou'rt sib kin to the sow,
But sibber to the deil, I trow;
An' what thy use can be, there's few
                    That can explain;
But naithing, as the learn'd allow,
                    Was made in vain.

Sure Nick begat thee, at the first,
On some auld *whin* or thorn accurst;
An' some horn-finger'd harpie nurst
                    The ugly urchin;
Then Belzie, laughin, like to burst
                    First ca'd thee *Hurchin*

Fok tell how thou, sae far frae daft,
Whar wind fa'n fruit lie scatter'd saft,
Will row thysel, wi' cunning craft,
                    An' bear awa
Upon thy back, what fairs thee aft
                    A day or twa.

But whether this account be true,
Is mair than I will here avow;
If that thou stribs the outler cow,
                    As some assert,
A pretty milkmaid, I allow,
                    Forsooth thou art.

I've heard the superstitious say,
To meet thee on our morning way,
Portends some dire misluck that day -
                    Some black mischance;
Sic fools, howe'er, are far astray
                    Frae common sense.

Right monie a hurchin I hae seen,
At early morn, and eke at e'en,
Baith setting off, an' whan I've been
                    Returning hame;
But Fate, indifferent, I ween,
                    Was much the same.

How lang will mortals nonsense blether,
And sauls to superstition tether!
For witch-craft, omens, altogether,
                    Are damn'd hotch-potch mock,
That now obtain sma credit ether
                    Frae us or Scotch fok.

Now creep awa the way ye came,
And tend your squeakin pups at hame;
Gin Colley should o'erhear the same,
                    It might be fatal,
For you, wi' a' the pikes ye claim,
                    Wi' him to battle.

ON A SPIDER

DESPOT like, see where it hings,
The fellest far of creeping things:
How artfully the glewy strings
       Enwarped are!
To thoughtless insects feet and wings
       A fatal snare!

When midges o' a merry sort,
About the window keep their court,
Their silly freaks, their wanton sport
       Gies him nae joy;
His steady aim is out to dart,
       And them destroy.

Full like to *him*, among mankind,
The gloomy, selfish, subtile mind,
Wha nae content nor glee can find
       In sang or whim;
Where interest's no wi' such combin'd,
       They're no for him.

And like to *them* the thoughtless chiel,
Despising Prudence' precepts leel,
Now here, now there, at random reel
       Thro' thick and thin,
Till hard and fast he's neck and heel
       In Ruin's gin.

To fate accumulated wrath,
This heavy hammer-head beneath,
I'll crush thee down to instant death,
       Vile, hateful creature!
To Ruin I thy den bequeath,
       Thou foe to Nature!

O cou'd I with an equal ease,
All murd'rers down to mummy squeeze!
Their tabernacles I wou'd breeze;
       Their souls I'd kick,
To wander in what forms they please
       Away to Nick.

THE HAWK AND WEAZLE

To town ae morn, as Lizie hie'd
    To sell a pickle yarn,
A wanton *Whiteret* she espy'd,
    A sportin at a cairn.
Alang the heath beskirted green,
    It play'd wi' monie a wheel:
She stood and dighted baith her een,
    An' thought it was the Diel
        She saw at freaks!

But soon her doubts were a' dismis't
    A gled cam whist'ling by,
And seiz'd the weazle:- ere it wist,
    'Twas halfway at the sky.
But soon the goss grew feeble like,
    And syne began to fa',
Till down he daded on a dyke,
    His thrapple ate in twa;
        Let him snuff that.

The weazle aff in triumph walks,
    An' left the bloodless glutton,
A warning sad to future hawks
    That grien for weazle's mutton.
So reprobates, that spitefu' cross,
    Decree their nibour's ruin,
Are aften forc'd, like foolish goss,
    To drink o' their ain brewin',
        Wha says its wrang.

ELEGY

LIZIE'S LAMENT FOR HER DOG LION

DEAR nibor Cummers, welcome here!
In sorrow ten times doubly dear!
Let each a sympathizing tear
      Let fa' bedeen,
For sic a breach this threty year,
      We hae na seen.

    It's no the loss o' cawf or cow,
Compells me thus to thraw my mou,
Nor loss o' nearest friends I trow,
      Cou'd thus confound me;
Mirk clouds o' woe my dog for you,
      Thick, thick surround me!

    Ye're now a cauld an' stiffen'd corse,
That was the herd o' ky an' horse:
An eke the safeguard o' my purse,
      Which now I fear!
Some knave wi' unrelenting force
      Will frae me tear!

    I'll ne'er forget while breath I draw,
That solemn night! ye mind it a'
That my auld father slipt awa,
      I hope to bliss;
The loss indeed was unco sma,
      Compar'd to this! —

    As 'mang my stacks I stood incog,
I saw the wicked, graceless rogue
Wi hasty steps come o'er the bog,
      Curse on the black!
* A sudden death he gi'ed my dog,
      Just in a crack!

Ah Lion! wale o' glossy tykes!
Nae mair ye'll spang the shoughs an' dykes;
Nae mair ye'll hap out o'er the sykes,
                    Wi tail erect:
Nor ever mair the beggar bykes
                    Gaur stan aback.

Thou, like mysel', a hatred bore,
To a' that lousy cantin' core:
Thou drove the miscreant's frae my door,
                    Just to my wish;
Whilk for the same till rinnin' o'er
                    I'd fill'd thy dish.

But now ilk ane withouten fear
May to my door-step venture near,
          An' o'er the floor an' grate mine ear
                    Wi gallin' mane,
Since him wha kept my ha' sae clear,
                    Is dead and gane!

Nae mair on you shall R——n cry on,
To urge the lazy stirks, an ky on:
Nor pauky weans again be tryin'
                    Wi' bread to win ye:
My G-d! my dog! my all! my Lion!
                    My heart was in ye!

While some wish'd this, and some wish'd that
Some sigh'd, some pray'd, while ithers grat;
Auld granny i' the peet-neuk sat
                    Wi' venom white ——
Wi meikle dole, she hostin spat
                    Her wrath and spite.

He was shot.

[7]

A PERIPATIAE

FORTUNE, I'll nae mair ca' thee bitch,
Base, hoodwink'd beldam, hag or witch,
Gude faith, thou'st lent me now a hitch,
      To glad my heart,
And set me up amang the rich,
      To play my part.

Nae mair I'll mix wi' duddy bykes,
O' cotter snools ydelvin dykes;
But sing and rant as best belikes,
      Wi' fok' in silk,
And scorn as dirt, the fool that fykes,
      For meal and milk.

What tho' to lear, I little claim,
I scarce can read or write my name,
Nor e'er was yet six miles frae hame,
      Yet, what the matter;
He never drees a deal o' blame,
      That gold can clatter.

What signifies or worth or parts,
Their boasted sciences or arts!
If emmet-like, a fellow scarts,
      Upon the earth,
He's just a gowk, 'tis gold my hearts,
      Brings wit and worth.

'Tis gold keeps a' the world alive,
To war it mak's the sodger drive;
It gi'es auld maids, o' fifty-five,
      The cheek o' youth;
And gars fause preachers aften rive,
      And hide the truth.

The fact is plain to half-shut eyes,
However some their minds disguise;
The wealthy man all ranks do prize
                As meritorious,
And equally the poor despise,
                As base inglorious.

For instance, if ye chance to meet
A man o' genius on the street,
Book-learn'd, a scholar made complete,
                Yet if he's duddy,
Wha deel will care ae head o' wheat
                For sic a body.

While on the ither han', if chance
Bring up the veriest stupid dunce,
Clad *a la mode*, as he'll advance,
                We crouchin' spirit,
The haflins blin', descry at ance
                The man o' merit.

I hope my auld acquaintance see
The reverence that's now due to me;
To joke thegither, and mak' free
                As we were wont,
On equal terms - O sir, 'twad be
                A sad affront.

Nae doubt they'll aim the spitefu' dart
O' rankling envy, at my heart;
And use malicious a' their art,
                To scandalize me;
But this I dont regard a f—t,
                'Twill ne'er surprize me.

I taylor was, some blockhead says,
Tho' now sae high my chin I raise;
An' botched a charming suit' o' claes,
                I made his dad,
Out on these lousy, early days,
                They put me mad.

O me, I never can endure,
To see relations at my door,
They're sic a 'sneakin'' pack and poor,
      They mak' me sconner;
When now th' address is, to be sure,
      'An' please your honour'.

I'm sure my daddy does perplex me,
My brither's visits sadly vex me,
My mither too, wi' kindness racks me,
      Auld stinkin' smoaker;
I often wish when she distracts me,
      The devil choak her.

O wad some tempest rise an' blaw,
The halewar o' them clean awa,
An' lare them deep, in Lapland snaw,
      Frae human sight;
Then I could caper, crousely craw,
      An' rant it right.

BAWSEY'S ELEGY,

AND EPITAPH - ON SEEING HER SKULL IN A DITCH

> *One portion of informing fire was given*
> *To brutes, the inferior family of heaven.*
> *DRYDEN*

AFTER a life o' labour past,
See whar my Bawsey's *craneum's* cast,
To bleach beneath the bitter blast,
   Trod in the clabor!
A sorry recompence at last
   For useful labour!

Lang thro' the fiels wi' me she flatter'd
In wheel-car, pleugh, and harrow splatter'd,
For whilk she freely fed unfetter'd,
   'Thro' Simmer bogs:
Now here and there her banes lie scatter'd,
   A' knaw'd wi' dogs!

When wi' a frien' it was my fate,
To stay in market rather late,
She'd, trottin, dousely fin' the gate,
   An' bring her master,
Hame at her ease to waiting *Kate,*
   Without disaster.

Therefore to gratify her *mane,*
I'll gather up her every bane,
And hide them frae the sun an' rain,
   In yon brae-head:
The following verse upon her stane,
   The fok' may read.

EPITAPH

O, stranger! whether high or low,
    Or clergyman or knave,
Know that this foggy stane doth show
    A noble filly's grave.

As sleek a meir as ever par'd
    The daisy frae the lee;
Wha thro' her life was better shar'd
    O' sense perhaps than thee.

O friend! let this engross thy thought,
    That life is but a day,
And man an' meir alike are brought
    To moulder in the clay.

The meir no more, but thou'lt exist
    Beyond the silent cell;
Either in heaven with the blest,
    Or with the damn'd in hell.

TO THE CUCKOO

Catch the first Cuckoo's vernal lay.
WARTON

AGAIN I hear thy hollow song,
　　Coo'd softly from the rural grove;
And Echo, lone, the glens among,
　　Repeating wild thy notes of love.

Once more to thee I fondly pay
　　The artless song, inspir'd by thine;
But I must own thy charming lay
　　Is worth a thousand such as mine.

Yet such as 'tis, O, take it kind,
　　(I sing to please no critic elf;
My simple sonnet, unrefin'd,
　　Flows only to amuse myself.)

Here, as by parent Lyle I rove,
　　Collecting Fancy's humble flowers,
Thy soothing song, from Granny's grove,*
　　Enlivens sweet my noontide hours.

The little minstrels fondly come,
　　And perching near thee, seem to say,
"For thee we have prepar'd a home,
Sweet *Laureate* of the flow'ry May."

* *Carngranny Grove*, where the Author reads
and muses with the greatest pleasure:
　　Nunquam minus solus,
　　Quam cum solus.

Is there, who deaf to thy soft note,
    Can call thee worthless, clam'rous fool?
Yes, there are such, full many a goat,
    That never conn'd at Nature's school.

When from lone tree, in sunny waste,
    On day serene thou'rt heard to sing,
He who the rapture cannot taste,
    Is but a cur tho' call'd a king.

Sweet bird, exulting, sing aloud,
    Thru' every green wood, glade and glen,
No more thou meet'st a *quarrelling crowd.*
    But TRUE UNITED IRISHMEN!*

While I can taste the sweets of May,
    And *rural muse* remains with me,
Inspir'd by thy harmonious lay,
    An annual song I'll pay to thee.

[NB: This verse only appears in the edition
printed in the <u>Northern Star</u> 15-19 May, 1797.]*

THE UNFORTUNATE FIDDLER

AE day a wan'ring fiddler, lame,
Upon a brig sat far frae hame;
Frae *tim'er case* alias frame,
         He drew's bread winner,
And on the range-wa' laid the same,
         Alas poor sinner!

    For lo, a wild unsonsy blast,
Down to the stream his fiddle cast;
Whilk hopeless on the current past,
         Wi' monie a hobble,
Leaving its master all aghast,
         Beset wi' trouble.

    While he, wi' monie a girn an' sigh,
Bewail'd his luckless destiny,
A countra' lout was drawing nigh,
         Wha frank and jolly,
Enquir'd at him the reason why
         Sae melancholy?

    Then bleering up, he 'gan explain
The sad occasion of his pain;
The 'big roun' tears,' like draps o' rain,
         Fell o'er his beard -
'Your *case* I pity,' quoth the swain,
         'Tis e'en right hard.

    Pity my *case* ye senseless bl—r!
Ye quite misunderstand the matter ——
Pity my fiddle, down the water!
         My *case* ye see't ——
'Humph,' quo' the fellow such ill-natur',
         The Deel gae wi't.

JAMIE'S DRONE

ATTENTION lend, ye rural train,
    Whilst I endeavour to rehearse
The praises o' a piper swain,
    In jingling hame-spun, knotty verse.

Nae mair ye bards exulting cra'
    'Bout Orpheus, and Eolian harps,
This chiel can easy ding them a'
    At either charming flats or sharps.

His melting sounds, his heavenly airs,
    Wou'd meliorate a heart of stone:
'Twould make a priest forego his prayers:
    The inchanting lilt o' Jamie's drone.

Then why to Italy ye gents?
    'Tis barefac'd like, and e'en a shame
'Mang beardless loons to waste our rents,
    When better music's had at hame.

Gude faith sic tours might weel be spar'd,
    Their silly springs - 'tis easy known,
Are anti-melody compar'd
    To the dainty dint o' Jamie's drone.

M'Laughlin[1] now may spare his brags
    An' that he's cow'd may frankly own:
M'Donnel[2] too, may slit his bags,
    An' bing sou-la to Jamie's drone.

Auld I——n[3] sleepy, slavering coof,
    May ever after now sing dumb,
Nor ever mair for weel creesh'd loof
    And drink to fairs and markets come.

M'C —b[4] too wi' tawny buff,
    May gae to bed and tak his nap;
Or i' the peet-neuk lie an snuff,
    But never mair erect his tap.

Had umqu'hile Spence[5] a listner been,
    Tho' weel he knew baith stap an tone,
He'd own'd himsel' fair dung I ween,
    By the lilt o' modern Jamie's drone.

In short, ye Fidlers, Pipers a',
    Or Highland bred or Irish fellows,
Maun never dare to cheep or bla'
    But break your bows an' burn your bellows.

To deck this charming minstrels brow,
    This British Pan[6] o' modern days,
Gae rustics haste and quickly pou
    A never-fading wreath o' bays.

And let it gracefully be plait,
    As weel he may the samen claim;
And syne we'll hae the Callan yet
    Enlisted wi' the sons o' Fame.

For a' the minstrels far an' near,
    If set in case were join'd in one,
Cou'd ne'er pretend I vow and swear,
    To the airy screed o' Jamie's drone.

1 A well known Scotch Fidler.
2 An eminent Highland Piper.
*3 A drowsy Fidler, well known in the
     neighbourhood of T——e P———k.*
4 Another snuff-consuming Musician of K—d.
5 An Irish Piper of the last century.
6 The Heroe of the Poem was an Englishman.

THE COUNTRY DANCE

O! ye douce fok, that live by rule,
Grave, tideless-blooded, calm an' cool,
Compar'd wi' you - O! fool! fool! fool!
                            How much unlike!
Your hearts are just a standing pool,
                            Your lives, a dyke!
                                            BURNS

COME muse, wha aft in merry tift,
Has ventur'd on the lyre;
        Wha aft frae laverocks in the lift,
Has snatch'd *poetic fire* :
        Come ye wha snug in hawthorn shade,
Sworn foe to spleen an' care,
        Enraptur'd e'ed the corny glade,
An' sung the SIMMER FAIR
                        Ance on a day.

        But Simmer fairs an' wabster louns *
Maun a' be laid aside:
        Or basted ribs an' broken crowns
Will aiblins us betide -
        We'll drap the silly theme at ance,
The merry maids an' swains,
        For singing quaint o' Habbie's dance,
Will thank us for our pains,
                        An' stroak our head.

* *The author was threatn'd within an inch of his*
life, for introducing the weavers of T——p——k,
into the SIMMER FAIR.

Aurora fair had quat the plain,
And harrowers lous'd their naigs,
    And seeds-men set, their supper taen,
To smoak an' rest their legs:
    Whan lads an' lasses blythe an' kin',
To Habbies wad repair,
    A few short hours to ease their min'
O warl'y moil an' care,
                An' dance that night.

    To fee them scourin' doun the dykes,
In *shauls* an' *aprons* glancin,
    An' here an' there the cottage tykes
Ay yelping at a chance ane:
    An' ithers rantin' o'er the braes,
Their hearts as light as cork-wood,
    An' whistling some o'er bogs an leas,
Ye'd true the fok were stark-wood
                On sic a' night.

    There at Hab's yard the *rural group*,
In merry mood convene,
    Whar some are at hap-step-an'-loup
While ithers put the stane:
    But soon the fiddle's dainty dint,
Recalls the *halewar* in,
    Whar pauky R—— wi' double squint,
Invites them to begin
                The sport this night.

    Come muse, we'll o'er to Habbie's hie,
The e'ening's calm an' fair
    At hame what need we snoaring lie——
An sican *pastime* there:
    We'll aiblins meet wi' L—— an' J——
That dainty, *social pair,*
    And get wi' them a dance an' crack,
Weel worth our gangin' there
                This bonie night.

Here some are come to crack an' joke,
An' toy amang the lasses;
    An' some to blether spit an' smoak,
An' bray like highland asses
    An' some to tauk o' ky an' corn,
Potatoes, sheep an' horses,
    An' some as thrawn wi' spleen an' scorn
As they'd been fed on curses
                Since their first day.

Now o'er the floor in wanton pairs,
They foot it to the fiddle;
    The maidens muster a' their airs
The young men skip an' striddle
    Ah! simple young things, ay beware
O' lurking INCLINATION!
    The clergy say, whan hobblin' there,
Ye're wabblin' temptation
                To ane anither.—

At *countra' dances*, jigs an' reels,
Alternately they ranted;
    Labs nimbly ply'd their rustic heels,
An' maidens pegh'd an' panted —
    Here *Rabin* lap wi' buxom *Jean*,
An *Liza* wi' her *Johney* ,
    While Willy in the neuk unseen,
Kiss'd *Meg* as sweet as honey
                To her that night.

Kings may roll in state, an' Lords
Enjoy their ill-got treasures;
    Compar'd to this their wealth affords
But superficial pleasures,
    Such happiness with pomp an' pride,
Is seldom ever seen,
    As here with rural swains abide,
In countra' barns at e'en,
                On sic an night.

O Burns! had I but half thy skill -
Thy bonie, silken stile,
    Description here shou'd flow at will,
In numbers smooth as oil:-
    But here I'll ask my reader's leave,
To make a short digression,
    It aiblins may in future prieve
To some a warnin' lesson
                Anither night.

    Behind a noest o' drawn strae,
I' the end o' Habbie's stack-yard:
    Poor simple Maggy a' night lay
Wi' Dick, that squintin' black-guard;
    Fair maidens oft may *sport* an' *dance*,
Their min's but little harm in,
    But ah! the dolefu' consequence,
Three quarters did determine
                To Maggy strang.

    Poor Meg! the scoff o' ilka chiel,
Forgrutten pale an' shabby,
    Now ca's about her lonely wheel
An' rocks asleep her babby!
    Frae her, ye maids a lesson glean,
An' trust yoursels wi' no man,
    'Bout *strae* or *bourtray neuks alane*
At dancings i' the gloamin,
                For fear o' skaith.

    Its weel wat I, the lee-lang night,
They neither fash'd nor tired;
    A gayer groupe, 'tis true ye might,
But neededna desired. -
    Here, far remov'd from city's strife,
Gay health an' young content,
    With pleasure gilds the shepherd's life,
While worldlings hearts are rent
                Wi' care an' fear.

Now rosy morn frae th' eastern steeps,
The shades o' night gan tirl,
    An' larks began wi' tunefu' cheeps,
Their morning springs to skirl:
    The lasses a' grown brave an' tame,
Alang the dewy fields,
    With kilted coaties hie them hame,
Escorted by the chiels
             In monie a pair.

    Thus ilka ane for hame o'erhies,
Some near, an' some a mile-hence:
    Whilst meagre R——b wi' heavy eyes,
Gies o'er the Barn to silence.
    Ill satisfy'd - in's *craving purse*,
The *Cappers* up he clinks!
    Then girnin', grumbling! slinks
           O'er next the Miltoun.

THE SIMMER FAIR

(As it is held in T____P____K, In the manner of Burns)

ON auld Hibernia's northern side,
    Whar corn and barley grow,
Whar pebbly, winding streamlets glide
    An' oxen graze and lowe;
Laigh in a vale there hauds a fair,
    As monie folks do ken,
Whar lads an' lasses ay repair
    The Simmer day to spend
            In sport and glee.

T'inspire the bardie at this time,
    Apollo be't thy care,
That he in Norland, measured rhyme,
    May sing the *Simmer-fair;*
Whar monie folks together hie,
    Baith married anes an' single,
Auld age and youth, wife, man an' boy
    A' hobbling intermingle
            In crowds this day.

Here grey-clad farmers, gash an' grave
    Drive in their sleekit *hawkeys;*
With monie a flee, auld-farrant knave,
    To sell their heftit *brockeys;*
An' Jockey louns, sae gleg an' gare
    Wi' boot be-deckit legs,
To glow'r an' drink, cheat, lie an' swear
    An' sell their glossy *naigs*
            Come here this day.

Here countra' chiels, dock'd aff compleat,
    Weel sheath'd in Sunday claes,
Sae trimly as they pace the street,
    In shoen as black as slaes; -
The lasses fain, come stringing in
    Frae a' parts o' the country,
Ilk ane as feat's a new made prin -
    Ye'd tak them a' for gentry,

Sae fine this day!
Here chapmen chiels unlock their packs,
    An' roun' display their toys;
Intent an' keen to wile the placks
    Frae silly jades an boys;
Ah! bonie young things have a care!
    Nor let their coaxin' trash
E'er claim your notice i' the fair,
    Or twin you an' your cash,
                But scant this day.

Here cantin varlets, thrawn an' cross,
    Wi' ballad singers skirle:
There blackguard boys at pitch-an-toss,
    Gar baw-bees nimbly birle;
Baith ginge' bread wives and tinkler jades,
    Stern W——s o' monie a texture,
With fo'k o' a' kinds, callings, trades,
    O! Heavens! what a mixture
                Comes here the day!

But hark! a *wabster* on the brig,
    Some how displeas'd a *suttor*,
Wha taks him in the wame a dig,
    An ca's him 'creeshy bluttor:'
Quoth he, to've been sae won'rous quick,
    'Ye neededna a fash'd man;
By that great Power that made Auld-Nick,
    'I'se hae ye bravely thrash'd man,
                This vera day!

Peace! (quoth the suttor) 'creeshy brock,
    'Or by my precious saul!
'Your poor, insipid, worthless bouk,
    'Shall in yon gutter spraul!
'Is he on earth d'ye think wad bear
    'Sic stroke - provoking smash?
'Then sirrah, cease! let's hear nae mair!
    'Or Saul I'll bravely smash
                'Your pate this day!'

Wi' that he raught him sic a rout
    Out o'er the dizzy crown,
As made thereat rthe claret spout,
    And laid the callan down:
A ploughman then, raught out a fist,
    Wi' wrathfu' choakin grapple,
And seiz'd the suttor ere he wist
    Just by the hairy thrapple —
        Held him that day.

Some hauds, an some as toughly draws,
    While cowardly dogs they craiked;
An' monie a ane, for ithers' cause,
    Gets bouk an banes weel paiked:-
But then had ye been there, an' seen
    How creature handled creature,
Ye might a sleekit baith your e'en,
    An' pitied human nature
        In sic a plight.

But soon the day's departing blink
    Gilds mountain, grove an' spire;
Ilk lad tips his ain lass the *wink*
    Syne outby a retire
Into the ale-house, warm an' snug,
    To court and quaff the brandy,
Whar kisses braid, frae lug to lug,
    Gang smack! like sugar-candy
        Sae sweet the night.

Now brandy punch, o' drink the wale,
    Skinks roun' in jugs and glasses;
The thoughtfu' swankies dinna fail
    To help the bashfu' lasses;
The jargon wild, frae Jockey's tongues
    Vociferous, endless roars;
While social chiels wi' cracks and sangs
    Beguile the wanton hours,
        O'er short the night.

Here *Liza* sits, wi' pride thrawn front,
    A bonie lass but fancy,
Wha, ere she wad a leman want,
    Taks *Jock* an' cares no wha see:
There Rabin oxters up his *Jean*,
    That's now as grey's a rat,
Wi' runkled brows and hollow ein,
    An' whiskers like a cat,
                Sae lang that night.

Much yet remains unsung, I swear,
    Right monie odd relations,
Descriptions that wad tire your ear,
    And far out-reach your patience:
For such a group as here was seen
    To grace the D—r's parlour,
Ye might, with weary steps I ween,
    Sought a' the crazy warl o'er
                Frae side to side!

But weel I wat they toom'd the horn,
    Till cocks began to craw —
Quoth some 'we'll catch a pour o' scorn,
    'except we haste awa:
'Our dads will gloom, and look right sour
    'That we're no sooner hame,
'Our Minnies flyte, an' girn an' glower
    'An' ferlie an' exlaim
                On us this day'.

Sae a' weel pleas'd, wi ae consent,
    They drowsy hamewards steer:
Some tak the road, and some the bent,
    Ilk lassie wi' her *dear:*
But some I wat, at nine months end,
    Wi hopeless dole, an' care,
Whan geer's a wrang, that winna mend,
    Will min' the Simmer Fair,
                An' curse that day.

Northern Star, September 1, 1792

SONNET

*Written on Monday, July the first, old stile, 1802,
being Templepatrick Fair-day, that year.*

WHILE half my neighbours now enjoy the fair,
    And give their vacant hours to social mirth,
Here, left a prey to dark desponding care,
    At home I muse me o'er the lonely hearth.

O how, just now, in Sam. M'Adam's room,
    The gabble rises unconstrain'd and free;
Poor solitary soul, may I presume
    That any there will waste a thought on me?

Perhaps some honest-hearted lad may say,
    "Lotharia likely, or ingenious Orr,*
What keeps the fellow from the fair to-day?
    I know he dearly loves the random splore."

Thus some are kind, whilst others quite uncivil,
Could wish, alas! my Bardship at the devil.

* *Mr Orr, the Poet.*

THE ROUGHFORT FAIR

A RUSTIC PARODY ON GRAY'S ELEGY

> *Reputation's a bug-bear to fools,*
> *A foe to the joys of dear drinking.*
> > *PHILLIPS*

> *Refreshment after toil, ease after pain.*
> > *MILTON*

THE day, at length, to evening's edge is come,
    And cools his axle in the western sea;
The mellow farmers drive their heifers home,
    And leave the fair to *social mirth* and me.

The glimmering candles light each festive room,
    And rural transport flies from nook to nook,
Save where the drunk man tumbles o'er the loom,
    And stagg'ring seeks some private place to puke.

Save that from yonder cobweb-mantled bed,
    The drunk-down jockey's sullen snores resound,
Who wishful turns, but turns in vain the head,
    For that repose which cannot there be found.

In farthest bed, with humble checquer hung,
    Heaving the rug, two social fellows rest,
Who gay till six o'clock, carrous'd and sung,
    But forc'd, alas! to give it up at last.

Of busy tongues the ever-varying roar,
    The song vociferous and wild horse-laugh;
Nay, all the transports of the *'random splore,'*
    Ne'er rouse these fellows from their bed of chaff.

In vain for them the blazing hearth may burn;
    Their wives in vain the supper may prepare;
In vain the children wish their sire's return,
    Expecting sweets and play-things from the fair.

Poor wives! how often are ye but deceiv'd
    With husband's promise when they go away;
For thus they tell you, and are still believ'd,
    'Upon my word, indeed, we will not stay'.

Howe'er, let not the shrew, with brazen face,
    In search of husband to the alehouse roam;
It plays the devil, and it brings disgrace;
    Far better stay and nurse their wrath at home.

Yet there are some, to all decorum dead,
    Like fiends will after to the ale-house fly;
Who boast the breaking of their husband's head,
    And how they can the social scene destroy!

And neighbours will impute to such the blame
    Of all the discord and domestic strife,
That feed, unsanctified, the wasting flame,
    Which still consumes the peace of marry'd life.

Can bitter scolding, kicks, and torn-out hair,
    Back to the mansion sweet agreement call?
Or can Contentment visit such a pair,
    Whose every day is one eternal brawl?

Perhaps in this gay festive place may lie
    The frothy schoolmaster, ere break of day;
Dull as a musket ball each turn'd up eye,
    That beam'd on truants the despotic ray.

But Knowledge to his eyes her ample page,
    Rich with the spoils of Time, did ne'er unroll;
Nature withheld from him the *noble rage* ,
    And froze the current of his stupid soul.

Full many a blockhead, impudent, and fool,
    The few intelligent are doom'd to bear;
Full many a worthless scoundrel keeps a school,
    And poisons intellects both far and near.

The stiff-neck formalist, with bigot breast,
    That vain new-light men ever keen controuls;
The subtle deist, held Religion's pest,
    Here fall together, all as drunk as owls.

Th' applause of sober people to command,
    The *'merry roar'* and bottle to despise,
Nay, on their feet like men to go or stand,
    Or e'en when fallen, up again to rise.

Their state forbids; but holds them here *incog.*
    In friendly Robin's hospitable shed;
Forbids to wade, all fours, thro' ditch and bog,
    Or tumble, zig zag, home to wife and bed.

The struggling pangs of vomiting to hide,
    And paley face from other's eyes to keep,
Some stragglers slip out to the garden side,
    Puke, yawn, and tumble over sound asleep.

Beyond the reach a while of grog and din,
    They sleep, and dream perhaps of wife and care,
Till waken'd sober, they again come in,
    And help their fellows to conclude the fair.

Now rouse ye, sleepers, from the bed of chaff,
    And set your rested bones once more erect;
This glass of stingo stout come quickly quaff,
    'Twill heal the head and all the man protect.

Tho' sick the stomach, and sore pain'd the head,
    To join their fellows they again are willing,
And many a plausive thing around is said,
    To make them board again the other shilling.

For who to hawk Economy a prey,
    The glee of such society would break;
Renounce the transports of the *old-fair* day?
    But want, alas! makes worthy fellows sneak.

Yet on some friend the moneyless may call,
  And, whispering, borrow half-a-crown or so;
Then, renovated, to the bottle fall,
  And rant and roar till bed-time, well or woe.

For thee who mindful of this drouthy corps,
  Dost in this crambo rhyme their tale relate,
A hundred times, I'm sure thou hast, and more,
  With such, till day-light, kept thy festive seat.

Haply some evil-minded folk may say,
  "Oft have we seen him drunk as drunk may be,
While far too narrow was the broad highway,
  Such stumbling, reeling to and fro kept he.

There, at the foot of yon romantic thorn,
  Whence issuing pure, the chrystal fountain flows,
We've seen him bathe his head full many a morn,
  And home to work, refusing all repose.

Oft o'er the sunny side of verdant *Lyle,*
  In pleasing melancholy rap'd, he'll rove,
And rustic madrigals compose the while,
  Singing them home by *Granny's* rural grove.

One morn we miss'd him on the flow'ry hill,
  Along the mead, and at his fav'rite tree;
A friend had ask'd him to partake a *gill* ,
  So in the whiskey house safe moor'd was he.

The evening following drunk, drunk indeed,
  From Wilson's sheban house he came along,
Still mutt'ring as he went with little heed,
  Something resembling the following song:"

THE SONG

Here 'lone I jog upon the face of earth,
    And on my fate tho' Fortune seem to frown;
Fair Nature smil'd upon my humble birth,*
    And sweet Contentment mark'd me for her own.

I'm somewhat versatile, but still sincere;
    Disdain to fawn or creep for selfish ends,
And Heaven, to chear me thro' this vale of care,
    Has given me *honest Damon*, best of friends.

O, let not Calumny the bard expose,
    His failings blazing in the face of day,
Because to whiskey shops sometimes he goes,
    To warm and moistify his tuneful clay!

* I was born on the 25th of blooming May, 1766.

LYLE'S HILL - A RHAPSODY

INSCRIBED TO DAMON

> *If I can be to thee*
> *A poet, then Parnassus art to me.*
>   *DENHAM*

O HAD I Denham's classic skill!
Or Dyer's soft, descriptive quill;
The beauties fair of verdant Lyle,
Shou'd echo round my native isle.
Come, Fancy, wanton, sportive lass,
Tripping o'er the velvet grass;
Bee-like, wand'ring far and near,
Come and aid thy votary here.
Come, thou solitary muse,
Wet thy flute with early dews,
And o'er these fertile flow'ry braes,
In mellow notes exalt the praise
Of Lyle, paternal hill, so long,
Gay Nature's pride, forgot in song.
Great Pope had Windsor's lofty groves,
Where ample Thames meand'ring roves;
Denham had *Cooper's Hill*, so fair,
And *Grongar* fell to Dyer's share;
While 'twas decreed for humble me,
Delightful Lyle, to sing of thee.

Here, while I sit upon thy brow,
What charming prospects meet my view;
Not haughty domes, unhallow'd towns,
Where noisy care true pleasure drowns,
But winding glens and stretching lees,
Sweet waving meads and blooming trees,
With here and there a farmer's home,
And wilds where flocks spontaneous roam;
Full many a bog and purple moor,
And many a lowly cot, obscure,
Where gracious heaven vouchsafes to bless
The inmates poor, with happiness.

[33]

Here while mine eye at random roves,
O'er spacious vales and nodding groves,
O, fair *Carngranny!* happy seat,
Of Peace and Truth the calm retreat;
Whate'er I hear, whate'er I see,
My heart still fondly turns to thee.
O'erjoy'd I gaze on every bower,
The haunts of many an idle hour;
Where first my "careless childhood" stray'd,
Where first I rustic strains essay'd -
And oft assiduous woo'd the muse,
For shamrock wreath to busk my brows.
Hail happy place! whose master kind,
Blest with a strong untainted mind;
Consistent, liberal, warm, humane,
Can look on sceptres with disdain,
And laugh at all the titled clan -
An independent, truly honest man.
See, along the furzy road,
The rustic schoolboys thoughtless plod;
Sportive, wanton, light as air,
Strangers to the world and care.
Happy youngsters, freely sport,
Life is fleet and very short;
Gayly spend your flowry May,
Sorrow's train are on the way;
Her motly group of cares and fears,
Haste to spoil your coming years;
Love leads the van of various strife,
Then follow all the ills of life.
Go, sweet youths, may learning's sun,
Blazing brightness, shine upon
Every bud of real merit,
Which your little breasts inherit;
And with warmth prolific nourish,
Till they into flowers flourish;
Gems of Genius, blooming clear,
To Science, Virtue, Erin, dear.

O how I love to lie, sweet Lyle,
Upon thy grassy brow, the while
Dan Phoebus drinks the morning dew,
Ascending up from Slavy-true;*
And eke to fit beneath yon rocks,
Beside the *thorn*, what time the flocks,
To cooling shades instinctive run,
To shield them from the mid-day sun.

Nor less I love o'er thee to stray,
When evening veils thy top with gray,
Sweet hill, I love thee all the day.
Just now 'tis morning clear and mild,
The blackbird, lark, and mavis wild,
The cuckoo and the constant rail,
Send soft delight on every gale.
See, on the road to town, a throng
Of Village shopmen, toil along,
Intent on gain, the fairest gem
In Nature's lap, is nought to them -
Stupid as stones, the vernal joy,
Is pass'd by such, unheeded, by:
And let them run, and let them ride,
Come, muse, we'll to the other side,
And see what pleasures wait us there,
Adown the southern valley fair.
See the landscape various spreading,
Simplicity the ditches leading,
Thro' mosses, fens, and woodlands hoar,
Down to *Neagh's* romantic shore.
Here in the shade of this whin bush,
All with golden blossoms flush,
Let us chant it at our ease,
And taste the cool refreshing breeze.
See at hand, that hoary dome
Solemn stands, Religion's home,
Where humble Christians weekly join,

* *A hill on the eastern coast of the County of Antrim.*

[35]

To sing their Maker's praise divine.
I greet the venerable place,
Basking in the rays of grace.
Hail, worthy man, who to the rock,
Leadst thy little thirsty flock,
And striking with the sacred *rod*,
The flint-dividing wand of God.
Obtains that *stream*, the sinner's cure,
Salvation's nectar, sweet and pure.
Happy people, thus instructed,
And thro' error's wilds conducted,
Fed with *Manna* from above,
Refreshing food of Heaven's love.
Meek and Lowly, let your tongue
Manifest that you belong,
Not to Ashdod's foul-mouth'd race,
But to him, the Prince of Peace.
O, the worthy * man revere
Who, with holy watchful care
For you pours his soul in ardent prayer.
Unlike the formal, puff'd professor,
And hypocrite, base transgressor,
Who all the week to Mammon pray,
Yet dare to preach on Sabbath day;
Who learn'dly wander in the dark,
Mastiffs dumb, that cannot bark.

　　Hush, my muse, now let's retreat,
Mid-day Phoebus' scorching heat
Flashes broad o'er hill and lee,
And sleepy langour seizes me.

* *The Rev. Mr. Patton.*

Accept, dear hill, the artless lay,
Which, due to thee, I grateful pay.
May piping herds, in future time,
Throughout the North, in rural rhyme,
Descant thy praise, while Echo sweet,
Doth all the various joy repeat:
When o'er thy slopes no more I roam,
But moulder in my *narrow home.*
Meanwhile, for many a coming spring,
In sight of thee I hope to sing;
Content my lowly shades among,
Still shielded from the vulgar throng,
And Envy's every busy medling tongue.

CRAMBO CAVE

TO DAMON

> *A rural, shelter'd, solitary scene.*
> *THOMSON*

BENEATH the northern brow of verdant *Lyle* ,
    Where fertile fields with green abundance wave,
Apart from clam'rous cities many a mile,
    Appears a rural cot, clep't *Crambo Cave.*

Here Nature simply, in contempt of Art,
    A rustic Poet to the world gave,
Who, wild as wood-lark, plays his *tuneful part,*
    Beneath the mossy roof of *Crambo Cave* .

Reader, if ever you shou'd pass that way,
    And curiosity sufficient have;
Albeit you relish and approve his play,
    He'll bid you welcome to his *Crambo Cave.*

But if you know yourself to be an ass,
    A blockhead thick-skulled, narrow, selfish knave,
Quick on your plodding, grappling business pass,
    Nor lose one moment here in *Crambo Cave.*

The draughty *cant* of avaricious rogues,
    Whose only *motive* is to *catch* and *save,*
Buy, sell and barter cows, sheep, horse and hogs,
    Is *antimelody* in *Crambo Cave.*

Let such for gold and gain's sake keep aloof,
    And to each other 'bout their dealings rave;
But never dare to persecute the roof -
    The muse-lov'd roof, and walls of *Crambo Cave.*

But come ye chosen, ye *selected few*,
  Who can be wise and witty, gay and grave,
The rustic owner doth solicit *you*,
  To come and see him oft in *Crambo Cave.*

And chiefly *Damon*, warmest heart of all,
  Thy chearful company he'd often crave;-
O come, obedient still to *Friendship's* call!
  Thou'rt ever welcome to his *Crambo Cave.*

     Crambo Cave, July 21, 1799

THE FAIRY KNOWE:

OR, DAMON'S BIRTH PLACE.

For love sincere, and friendship free,
Are children of Simplicity.
                                        LANGHORNE

'WILT thou go,' says Damon, 'and behold the spot
     Where stood the cottage, where thy friend was born;
Indeed the place is nearly now forgot,
     But I still know it by the *hedge of thorn.*

It's humble site the ruthless plow has torn,
     Eraz'd and fertiliz'd the little floor;
Where lonely *Craiks*, among the waving corn,
     Now hatch their young, and feed and cry secure.'

Well pleas'd, my Damon, I will go along,
     And on thy scene primeval muse an hour;
There give thy friendly ear a simple song,
     And sigh with thee for the deleted bower.

          Yes, upon the vernal brow
          Of the humble fairy knowe,
          We will sit and trace the spot
          Where stood thy father's tufted cot.
          The dwelling where thy infant sight
          Open'd first on chearful day;
          Now, by Time's assiduous flight,
          All o'erthrown, and brush'd away.
          While Memory essays to draw
          From Oblivion's wasting maw,
          All the little list of things
          Fluttering Fancy flaps her wings,
          And to Imagination's view,
          Builds the long lost bower anew.
          I see the little opening door,
          The useful shelf, and chest and chair,
          Thou an infant, on the floor,

Snatching play things here and there.
I see thee to the fairy knowe
At noontide with thy playmates ramble,
Pluck the gowan from its brow,
And for the yellow trifle scramble.
I hear thy mother kindly call
Home her son at Evening's fall,
And telling of the *Wiricow,*
That nightly haunts the fairy knowe;
I see thee court thy father's smile,
Seated on his weary knee,
When return'd from twelve hours' toil,
To his cottage, rest, and thee.
The scene is fled! the waving corn
Now rustles o'er the *sod,*
Where by the well-known hedge of thorn,
The lowly dwelling stood!
Thus Ruin's bessom sweeps
The works of man away;
And hoar Oblivion after creeps,
And blots our mortal day:
The castle and the cottage are
Alike their crumbling prey.
Thus simply I've berhym'd the place
Where *Damon* had his birth,
Who is, of all the human race,
My dearest friend on earth.
Long since thy honest heart and mine
Together fondly grew:
So Damon dear this verse is thine,
And thine its Author too.

October 13, 1797

NOVEMBER

TO DAMON

Now hoary Winter, cauld an' keen,
    Erects his wither'd tap ance mair;
And, shivering owre the naked scene,
    Flouts ragged rustics unco fair;
        Wha, ne'ertheless, on Hallowe'en,
        About the hearth sae trig an' clean,
        Reckless o' frost, or sna, or rain,
        Agree to burn their nits again;
        While fairies fleet their gambols play,
        Thro' mony an eldrich glen an' brae.

In pairs, before the ingle now,
    The mystic nits are laid alang,
And presently they a' tak' lowe,
    And blink and burn, some right, some wrang
        (O, Superstition! crazy fool!
        Thin, thin is worn thy silly school;
        For Learning's soul-exalting ray
        Has rescued mankind frae thy sway
        Except at times, when rural glee
        Invites thee back to laugh at thee.)

The auld gude man, indifferent, sees
    The pastime that he ance held dear;
While younkers eye the dancing bleeze,
    Wi' counterfeited hope and fear.
        An' social graunie taks her smoak,
        Laughs wi' the lave, and clubs her joke;
        Gies her auld mou the youthfu' twine,
        Waesucks, to think on a lang syne,
        And tells how happy she has been,
        A-burning nits on Hallowe'en.

O, Damon, while the minutes flee
 On silent wing, unfelt, unseen,
Wilt thou again come down to me,
 And laugh at Folly's Hallowe'en.
   How thy auld wrinkled dow and mine,
   Wad sit and plot, and girn, and whine;
   And burn prophetic nits forsooth,
   Insulting age wi' glaiks o' youth!
   The L—d preserve us frae their clutches,
   The grey-beard, auld-smell'd, wither'd witches.

A social jug here waits my frien',
 And eke the heel o' an auld cheese,
That's now as onie raddish keen,
 And canna fail, I think, to please.
   Here, hid apart frae vulgar strife,
   And a' the din o' married life;
   While Friendship smiles upon our lot,
   And closer draws the mutual knot,
   We'll sit and crack till midnight hour,
   Then gae to bed and sleep secure.

ACROSTIC - TO DAMON

Just such a bond of union, as of old,
Saul's son and David did together hold,
Our hearts hath bound in an eternal tie,
And which to loose, we time and man defy.
Heaven withholding wealth, to make amends,
More to endear our state, hath made us friends,
Never to separate, our names here stand,
United closely by the Muse's hand.
While blooms the hawthorn in the flow'ry vale,
Enriching sweetly every passing gale;
In meadows moist, while bending oziers sew
Love-breathing shepherds where to sigh their woe;
Like as our souls in mutual friendship join'd,
The reader here our names enwarp'd will find.
Life's a short passage, down a doubtful steep,
Hence Death, black monster, with unpitying sweep,
In a few fleeting years, short months, or days,
Our humble station from this scene will raise.
Ah, when the gloomy hour at last draws nigh,
Might we together up to Heaven fly,
Might we together but be call'd away,
Softly, to regions of eternal day;
Secure, we'd scorn the meagre traitor's dart,
Our only greatest fear, that we should part.
O, if my soul should first from earth get free,
Not even in heaven could it happy be,
Nor relish bliss till thou coulds't share't with me.

A JONSONIAN FRAGMENT

OCCASIONED BY A VISIT TO MR BURNS, IN SPRING, 1794

> *I sing the brave adventure of two wights,*
> *And pity 'tis I cannot call 'em knights.*
> *BEN JOHNSON.*

'TWAS at that season of the turning year,
When smiling Spring puts hoary Winter hence,
From old Hibernia's rural fields and groves,
Far to his frigid mansion in the North;
Where, o'er the icy hills, and wastes of snow,
His meagre, cold domestics shivering dance,
In wildly frightful measures round the pole;
While from the southern sky, the balmy power,
Breathing soft fragrance o'er our fertile plains,
Awakes the transports of the vocal grove,
And lonely Echo, from her hollow cave,
On fluttering zephyr, down the winding glen,
Again, exulting, sends the song of joy.

'Twas then, abandoning the din of business,
That I resolv'd to see the *Land of Cakes* -
To feast my eyes upon these fairy scenes,
So oft by Caledonian poets sung.
But thou, sweet *Burns*, the Scottish Shakespeare,
Of modern days, I chiefly long'd to see,
With my design, thus ripe for execution,
By one accompanied, an *only friend, *
I bade farewell a while to care and cottage,
And to the place of embarkation sped.
Arriv'd, the remnant of that day was spent
In fond impatience, looking o'er the ocean,
Much wondering what the next day would produce,
That night beneath the hospitable roof
Of kind F——e we slept. The morning smil'd,
And hoarse-throat sailors hail'd us straight aboard.
Propitious gales, from Erin, land of bogs,
In three hours took us to the other side.

[45]

Now on the Scotian shore our feet we found,
What strange ideas throng our busy minds,
As *Morven's* rugged hills around us rise!
Her oaken groves, old Nature's handy-work,
Romantic glens, and ancient ivied ruins,
The seats of former grandeur, here and there,
In gloomy prospect met our wond'ring eyes.
Away we steer from Patrick's ancient port,
Now over-stretching deserts, gloomy, sullen,
Where far apart from any human dwelling,
Except, perchance, a shepherd's *heathy booth*,
Forsaken Solitude, abruptly frowning,
Associates ever with the nibbling sheep.
Now thro' sweet vallies, winding picturesque.
Where, down descending from the hoary hills,
Thro' fertile farms and prosperous villages,
Clear rivers roll their tribute to the sea;
Sweet smiling villages, where hospitality,
Familiar, kind, the weary traveller chears.
This two days morn and evening past; the third
Saw us well moor'd in Dumfries ancient town.
Soon as I knew his Bardship liv'd convenient,
I for him sent, nor could I wait till morning.
I sent - he came - but O, ye heavenly powers!
What strange emotions ran o'er all my soul,
When I beheld the Ayrshire poet's face!
And is it he? - I look'd and look'd again,
And scarce could credit give my wondering eyes.
He spoke - I listen'd with a pleasing awe,
Attention hung on every thing he said.
O yes, Hibernians, I beheld the *Bard*,
Old Scotia's jewel, and the muse's darling,
Whose matchless lays, despite of wasting time,
Shall to the last of earthly generations,
Remain old Nature's boast and Scotia's pride.

* *Damon.*

LINES FROM DAMON

Oft have I prov'd the labours of thy love.
BLAIR

O SAM, thou learn'd me first to mark
  The dancing glow o' Burns's fire;
And gied to me that dainty spark,
  That mak's me ay his sangs admire.
Ere first my bosom to thy ain
  Was kent, I pass'd a tasteless time:
Wi' care an' crouds I liv'd alane,
  Nor thought of Burns, nor thee, nor rhyme:
But Friendship saw, an' gat a string,
  Ane teugher far than tug or tether,
Which Time can ne'er assunder wring,
  And ty'd our honest hearts together.
Now Nature's beauties glad my heart,
  Let Spring or Summer deck the land,
Or Autumn load her patient cart,
  Or Winter whirl it great and grand.
Aft I peruse that Minstrel sang,
  Sweet *Edwin* sung, o' bards the best;
The wild brook babbling down alang,
  The shepherd's pipe and a' the rest.
D'ye mind that bonie morn of May,
  As owre the hills to town we strode,
Ye tauld me scraps o' that sweet lay;
  And a' its beauties to me shew'd;
  Ere since I'm wed to poesy;
And tho' my skills but unco scarce,
  My crambo I can croon wi' thee,
And vent my rustic thoughts in verse.
  Aft wand'ring pensive o'er the hill,
I feel the wild romantic glow;
  Drink Nature's health at every rill
And sowf a sang on every knowe.
  Here corbies spread their sable wings,
And croaking fly from brae to brae;
  Poor lambs, defenceless, timid things,

Are made their unresisting prey!
    Ah, Cruelty! thou bloody shark,
Whether we roam earth, air, or sea,
    Thy crimson course we're sure to mark,
And hear the frightful croak o' thee!

                    DAMON

EPISTLE TO L—M——,

A BROTHER BARD

WHILE yellow Autumn hies apace,
An' ripening fiels' and blighted braes
    Confess the waining year:
To you my frien', in Burns's way,
I thus sooth up a roundelay,
    My drooping spirits to chear.
Ah me! dear L—, the season's fled -
    The flow'ry months o' joy;
The tuneless wood an' ravish'd mead
    Proclaim the winter nigh.
Come see now, with me now,
    How *Flora* quits the lees;
Whilst *Boreas* before us
    Is stripping all the trees.

But what need I in tears complain,
Or grief beset, in lowly strain,
    Thus pour my plaint of woe:
When 'tis the fate of all on earth, -
When 'tis for this we have our birth,
    On *terra* here below.
All flesh is like the grassy vest
    That haps the Simmer brae,
When winter cauld the plains arrest,
    It withers straight away.
The youngest, the strongest,
    Return alas! they must,
With oldest an' boldest,
    At all events to dust.

What boots it here to grasp at *rules?*
Even all the knowledge of the schools
    Is but a poor resource!
For ay the mair that ye're inclin'd,
To read this *volume* o' mankin',
    Ye'll like it still the worse.
Aroun' the warl, look an' stare,
    An' tell me if ye can,
Where I may find in truth sincere.
    Ten social, honest men;
But mask all, each rascal,
    Deceiving an deceiv'd:
I true Sir! I vow Sir!
    There's few to be believ'd!

I've often read, an' often heard,
That *poortith* for the rustic bard,
    Doth ever lie in wait:
While partial *Fate* profuse bestows
On wicked sons o' tasteless *prose,*
    Even kingdoms, crowns an' state!
    My mind to me's a kingdom wide,
    Nae mair I wish or want:
Tho' poortith on my riggin ride,
    I'm happily content.
Tho' tost aft, an' crost aft.
    By faithless, foolish fok',
I meet still, an' greet still,
    Misfortune with a joke.

My life as like the chrystal rill
That wimpling flows, with sweetest thrill,
    Adown the gowany brae:
That ceaseless frae its rocky source,
Pursues its pebbly, winding course,
    Still murmuring to the sea
Amid the landscape, lonely here
    I up my whistle bla',
As down life's *cruked* path I steer,
    To frighten care awa.
With L——e whiles, a book whiles,
    To pass a happy *hour;*
I'm careless an' fearless
    How faithless Fortune lour.

Wi' glowan heart I'm right content
To see your name wi' mine in *prent,*
    In humble *rural rhyme:*
The swains unborn of other days,
Will jocund chaunt our simple lays,
    Adown the vale o' time:
Whilst you an' I neglected sleep
    Aneath some mossy stone;
Where nightly owls their vigils keep,
    And wae-worn turtles moan!
Reposing, there dosing,
    We'll wear the years away,
Baith roun'ly, an' soun'ly,
    Until the Judgment day.

Come haste my brither! in a clap
Unhouse your dapple-winged *crap*,
    An' mount wi' right good will:
Withouten either whip or spur,
He'll tak the road with airy birr
    An light on *Parnas' Hill,*
Already on its airy height,
    I see ye tak' your stand!
The blissful vales come full in sight,
    Of fair Arcadia's land
    Haste bring then, an'sing then
Ilk ferlie ye saw there —
    From views there what news here?
Come haste an' let me hear!

                  Carngranny, August 27, 1791

EPISTLE

*TO MR R****T B***S*

SWEET Scottish Bard! still as I read
Thy bonie, quaint, harmonious lays,
    I aft exulting bless thy head,
That weel deserves to wear the *bays*.

    " 'Tis long indeed since Scotia's plain
Cou'd boast of such melodious lays -"
    'Twou'd take, O Burns! an able pen
To match thy merit and due praise.

    Tho' Allan Ramsay blythly ranted,
An' tun'd his reed wi' merry glee;
    Yet faith that *something* ay he wanted,
That makes my Burns sae dear to me.

    Possest of sic uncommon skill,
Horatian fire at command;
    Thou, easy can'st teach *Dogs* at will,
What's human life at ance to scan!

    An' whan got in a merry vein,
Thou tun'st thy reed to *auld Scotch drink*:
    I've aften lang'd, an' lang'd again
To see my Burns's *social wink*.

    L—d man, I aften think on you!
Whan to the kirk our saints forgather!
    A hypocrite, senseless crew!
It puts ane mad to hear sic blether!

    Likewise the *Esculapian rout,*
Vile sinners! faith thou has na spar'd them:
    I wish this fourscore years a' out,
Baith you an' I may disregard them.

Your bonie lines on *Halloween,*
I aften read whan I'm at leisure;
    The weel depicted, countra' scene
Affords to me, the greatest pleasure.

    HOMER * I've read, an' VIRGIL too,
With HORACE, MILTON, YOUNG and GAY.
    Auld SPENCER, POPE and DRYDEN thro',
Sweet THOMSON, SHENSTONE, GOLDSMITH, GRAY.

    I've aften read their pages a'
An' monie mair o' deep ingine:
    But frae a' the verses e'er I saw,
Your *Cotter* fairly taks the shine.

    Your *Dream* and *Vision* mak me fistle:
Right monie a time I'm made to laugh
    At the comic turn o' ilk *epistle,*
Likewise your *ecclesiastic cawf.*

    And wha the devil wadna praise ye,
That has impartial, read ilk *sonnet* ,
    That ye hae sung to *mouse* an' *daisy,*
An' *louse* upon my *lady's* bonnet!

    An whan ye bid *farewell* to Ayr,
Your wonted vales an' verdant hills,
    An' to your *brethren* o' the *square* ,
With warmest throws my bosom fills.

    Than greening wife mair lang I think,
To get my e'en for ance upon ye,
    To see ye smile an' laugh an' drink
Wi' you in antient Caledonia.

* *Translations only.*

The road is lang an' unco driegh,
And roaring seas do intervene;
    And cauld-rife mountains, wild an' hiegh,
Erect their joyless brows atween.

    But yet that *hour* may come to pass,
That in some thrang perchance I'll see ye,
    An' hap'ly treat ye to a glass,
An' likely grow familiar wi' ye.

    Farewell sweet bard! may Heavenly powers,
Frae a' that's ill for ay deffend ye;
    Health, joy an' peace be ever yours;
And happiness for ay attend ye.

    And when your spirit quits her clay,
May angels be her *dear convoy*
    To regions of eternal day —
To fountains of eternal joy.

LINES, ADDRESSED TO THE REV J—— P——

Inclosing the foregoing

WITH scientific eye, exploring space,
Pursuing far the philosophic race,
    From Mercury's disk to utmost Saturn's ring,
Wilt thou, my P——r, fraught with classic lore,
And soul *Newtonian*, qualified to soar,
    Now condescend to hear thy poet sing?
In mournful strain, the death of tuneful BURNS,
That long as July's * fatal month returns,
    To these sad eyes the tears shall spring amain,
And lonely *Echo* catch the woeful wail,
In broken accents, floating on the gale,
    For him whose like we scarce can see again.
Yes, you, with candour, will the strain attend,
Of him who boasts that he can call you friend.

* *Mr Burns died July 21st, 1796.*

VERSES

COMPOSED IN THE HERMITAGE OF GREENMOUNT, SEPT. 3rd, 1801

ADDRESSED TO MRS. THOMSON

Sweet is the breath of vernal shower,
The bees collected treasure sweet,
Sweet music's melting fall, but sweeter yet,
The still, small voice of gratitude.
GRAY

SWEET GREENMOUNT, hail! thy vernal name
    Is music on my artless tongue;
This day from *Crambo Cave* I came,
    To greet thee with a simple song.

But chiefly to revisit thee,
    My patroness, and generous friend,
And E——'s cherub face to see,
    My course I here did hither bend.

Now in thy hermitage, apart,
    I tune my rustic reed once more;
And, wondering, bless that head of art,
    That plann'd the strange romantic bower.

Shenstonian fire thy bosom warm'd,
    With all *his* Leasowes-sketching glow -
And to see this curious grotto form'd,
    His genius hover'd down below.

Sure Heaven alone inspires the mind,
    With every first-rate virtue fair;
To whom the Indian seas resign'd
    Their coral beds, and beauties rare.

While other travellers but amuse
    Us with a stale description cold;
Here we the Indies may peruse,
    And half their curious things behold.*

Here ART and NATURE kindly meet,
    While elegance of taste refin'd,
Enjoys the mental banquet, sweet,
    That dignifies the enlighten'd mind.

Here Innocence may sleep secure,
    Poor exile, o'er the world driven;
And Piety, with fervour pure,
    May waft her holy wish to heaven.

Delightful place! where I could long,
    Did time allow me, lingering stay;
And musing, hum my artless song;
    But something whispers, "come away."

Permit your bard, ere he depart,
    To breathe one ardent, honest prayer,
Which flows spontaneous from the heart,
    That Heaven can witness is sincere.

O Thou, from whom all bliss descends,
    Smile on this thriving place, I pray,
Protect my patronizing friends,
    And keep misfortune far away.

And, O! thou power omnipotent!
    My *namesake patron* bless alway,
With health, and peace, and sweet content,
    Till lengthened life's remotest day.

* *Alluding to the wonderful collection of Indian
curiosities now at Greenmount.*

Now curious grot I'll take my leave
    Of you, and home again repair,
To parent *Lyle* ,and *Crambo Cave,*
    And friends that wait my coming there.

There, ever as I'll stray in view
Of thee, kind Greenmount, I'll renew
My wishes for thy happiness,
And all thy generous inmates bless.

TEMPLEPATRICK'S ADDRESS
TO THE RIGHT HONOURABLE
MY L—D T———N.

YE'RE welcome hame my honour'd youtl
May health an peace attend ye;
   And Fortune ever kind an' couth,
Frae every ill defend ye:
   Frae wisdoms law, and seraph truth,
By which as yet ye stand ay,
   May nae deceitfu' wanton mouth
Presumptive, dare to bend ye
         I humbly pray.

This while I've been in *sober* vein,
   Distraction maist had smoor'd me;
But your gay presence back again
   Has to mysel' restored me,
Therefore the best my wa's contain,
   Shall come upon your board ay;
And faith o' nibour touns there's nane
   That better can afford ay,
         On onie day.

'Tis true, to vie wi' London toun,
   Gude kens I'm no sae fancy,
Yet here ye may walk up and doun,
   Whan Simmer drys my causway:
My Sires wi' liart, uncover'd croun
   Will gladly meet and bless ye;
My daughter's fair, in russet goun,
   Wi' *courtsies* will caress ye
         As ye gae by,

O! wad ye henceforth stay at hame
    Content wi' your ain ha',
Nor ever mair impair your frame
    By roavin' far awa:
Then I'd exult in great acclaim -
    Wad cock my crest an cra!
And norland bards on trump o' fame,
    Your praises loud wad bla',
            Frae bank to brae.

Heaven send, and soon some lady blyth,
    Deservin' to your bosom,
And may your mutual flame ycyth
    And in sweet bairnies blossom:
May grey-beard Time wi' sweeping scythe,
    An' death wi' aspect awsom
Gae some whar else an' levy tythe,
    An spare the happy twasome
            Right monie a day.

L—d lend ye langest life, and sense
    To fill your honour'd station;
And may ye drive corruption hence,
    Wi' fraud an' dissipation:
Inspir'd by your chearing glance,
    I'll yet turn out in fashion,
An be as trig a toun perchance,
    As onie in the nation
            Some future day.

TO CAPTAIN M'DOUGALL, CASTLE-UPTON:

WITH A COPY OF THE AUTHOR'S POEMS.

KIND sir, accept the artless strains,
    Of one who wishes well to you;
One who reveres old Scotia's plains,
    And all her lads and lasses too.

Oft wild-wood Fancy restless roams,
    Among her well-sung, classic braes,
Where our forefathers had their homes,
    The hardy sons of other days.

And still when inspiration comes
    To my night thoughts, and mid day dreams,
'Tis from her breezy, willowy holms,
    Romantic groves and winding streams.

Indeed Fate seems to have mistook
    The spot at first design'd for me;
Which should have been some flow'ry nook
    In Ayr, or on the banks of Dee.

I love my native land, no doubt,
    Attach'd to her thro' thick and thin;
Yet tho' I'm *Irish* all *without* ,
    I'm every item *Scotch within* .

As you may easily remark,
    When looking thro' these rustic lays,
In *costume Scotch,* o'er bog and park,
    My hame bred Muse delighted plays.

You'll find too, sir, when to peruse
    These artless rhymes you condescend,
Sufficient that demands excuse,
    But little that you can commend.

Of this, however, still be sure,
    That with a zeal heart-felt and fervent,
While life and health with me endure,
    I'll be your grateful, humble servant.

Jan.31,1806

EPISTLE TO THE REV. JAMES GLASS, M.A.

Will men of sense and taste approve my strain?
                                            WILKIE

DEAR GLASS, wilt thou accept a sang,
A simple lilt, no vera lang,
  In artless, Scottish style?
Compos'd beside a lonely thorn,
That monie a cauldrife blast has borne,
  Upon the brow of Lyle;
Whar I full oft frae blockhead's din;
  To Solitude retire,
My rustic madrigals to spin,
  And tune my humble lyre;
While larks fleet, frae parks sleet,
  On floating pinions rise,
High touring and pouring
  Wild music thro' the skies.

Here I can sit in rural state,
And smile on a' the *little great,*
  These buzzards o' the creation,
Wha chasin' modest merit still,
Frae shore to shore, frae hill to hill,
  Extend their devastation.
That they are rich and I but poor,
  I dinna care ava:
Yet its no easy to endure
  Their rude insulting jaw!
The ninny see, when guineas he,
  Can jingle in his pocket,
An' suit new, his snout how
  Provokingly he'll cock it!

What tho' sic gude-for-naithing foes;
To mar our innocent repose,
      Full monie schemes invent;
Despite o' a' their power and art,
Ay conscious o' the honest heart,
      We'll try to rest content
Is there amang them a' can taste
      Like us, the kindling dawn,
The raptures o' the breeze waste,
      Or *daisy sheeted* lawn?
But wealth Sir, we've health Sir,
    An' Nature's sweets are free;
To feel then, sae weel, then,
    Is rowth to you an' me.

What signifies blin' Fortune's frown?
What tho' we wander up and down,
      Frae Grandeur far exil'd?
Unpetted by the gaudy throng,
Sweet Nature's various scenes among,
      We chant our *"wood-notes wild."*

The linnet's or the mavis' lay,
    Is sweeter I'll engage,
When carol'd frae the blooming spray,
    Than chanted frae a cage.

Thro' woods now, whar buds now,
    On thorns begin to smell,
We'll stray wild, and play wild
    Conceits, to please oursel.

O, sir, quat politics an' news!
To other themes invoke your muse;
   Sic as by Leven's side,
Ance streekit on the downy grass,
Ye sung to please a thrawart lass,
   An' win her for your bride.
Had I your powers for rural sang,
  Here ilka stream and vale,
Ilk hawthorn glen an' meadow lang,
  Shou'd lear my tuneful tale;
You'd see then, ilk tree then,
  To bloom the dykes alang;
The bowers with flowers,
  Shou'd blossom in my sang.

Now, sir, I'll quat my roundelay,
And whether it be found to hae
   Beginning, middle, en';
Or whether downright nonsense, dull,
Or prose run mad, or what you will,
   I neither care nor ken.
Nae rules I heed, I rhyme awa,
  Tak' what the musie gies me;
Sae if this may an answer draw
  Frae you, 'twill greatly please me,
Whilst I, sir, when dry, sir,
  The whisky stoup can drain,
Your servant most fervent,
  An' true, I here remain.

Lyle, April, 1796

ANSWER

TO PAINE'S "AGE OF REASON."

O argument, blasphemous, false, and proud.
                              MILTON

Your ruin, Tom, I never meant;
I'm griev'd to hear your banishment,
But pleas'd I'll be when you relent.
                              SWIFT

DEAR TOM, I have read your production all over,
With the greatest attention, but cannot discover,
From the first to the last, of right reason a tittle,
Or argument either, the worth of a spittle:
For reason does all your assertions despise,
As foolish conjectures, blasphemy and lies.

But what could provoke you to *write* such a babble,
And *print* it, to poison the minds of the rabble?
The devil - who flew to your weather-beat sconse,
After frighting away your own dear *Common Sense,*
(For any such lodger a damn'd deal too hot,)
On your brain this base trifle of trifles begot:
Contemptible trifle - O had it in wind
Pass'd from your republican *section* behind,
Or e'en like a bull-frog kept croaking within,
'Twou'd have sav'd your poor soul from a world of sin,
'Tis likely, perhaps, you esteem it a farce,
That there's any such thing as a hole in your a——
Because that, alas! you cou'd only be told it,
A palpable *hearsay*, you ne'er could behold it!

Sure Watson did all his great powers prostitute,
By endeavouring your infidel page to refute;
The tenth of his learning it did not require,
To discover that you were an impudent l—r;
Which, to the author of such diabolical stuff,
In sight of all good men, was answer enough.
To such a dilemma of devilishness driven,
After vexing the world, you'd next be at heaven!
With its constitution set mortals at odds,
Bawl out 'Revolution, and down with the Gods!'

Poor wasp of Commotion, the foot-ball of Fate,
A fugitive driven from state unto state,
Still panting to join the political fray;
With horrible wars, guilt and gibbets to stay;
Unknown in the season of peaceful repose,
Except by exciting cross parties to blows;
Thy life, O poor Paine! is a pitiful scene
Of inverted philanthropy, madness and spleen.

ELEGY ON R——— I————

COME a' ye yonkers o'er the dale,
Let grief a while your mirth assail;
Death wi' a smite o' his lang flail
      Has reach'd his head,
An' gien us a' cause to bewail
      R——— I——— dead.

  Our Norland lasses may look wae,
And glowr about wi' aspect blae:
Poor Rab, that erst was heard to play
      Wi' lively screed,
Is ruthless flung to worms a prey
      Amang the dead!

  He was nae man o' meikle lear -
O' countra lore he had his share,
Wi' deep disputes he didna care
      Ava to meddle:
In short he kent but little mair
      Than play the fiddle.

  Some said he cou'dna play'd a reel
As true as monie anither chiel;
I thought his music did as weel,
      For a' their blethers,
T' inspire a countra' fellow's heel,
      As onie ither's.

  Wi' A———n monie a day he jinket,
An' monie a penny frae him clinket;
He's fixt his specks, an' gravely winkit,
      An' spungt the cash!
But never ran awa to drink it,
      Like him, fool hash!

He was nae drinker, ne'ertheless
He dearly lo'ed a social glass;
But if he chanced to transgress
      And bounds o'er shoot,
It chang'd the fidler to the ass,
      That lang-ear'd brute.

Ah R——n! aft thy chearing fiddle
Has made the wee anes twine and widdle,
An' youthfu' spunkies skip and striddle,
      In barns at e'en
Wi' maidens jimp about the middle;
      Baith blithe an' keen.

Mysel' I've aften been right vogie
To hear thee skirl up Bally bogie;
Tho' some loons ca'd thee selfish rogue ay,
      An' catch the money,
Thou kept thy ain auld sleepy, jog ay
      nor minded ony -

A lie like clatter ance gaed roun',
That Rab, when tempted wi' a crown,
To please, O fye! a graceless loon,
      Ae Sunday night,
Sat down and play'd tune after tune
      Till clear day-light.

Now pithless lies that artfu' arm
That taught the nice extended thairm,
Wi' music's silver, magic charm
      To thrill sae clear;
The youthfu', tunefu' heart to warm
      An' age to chear.

He's dead an' burry'd! - let him lie,
And if misconduct ye do spy,
Ah! fling it in oblivion by,
      Ye cantin' core!
He has an awfu' judge on high
      To come before!

EPISTLE TO MR R————, BELFAST;

ON RECEIVING A FLATTERING EPISTLE FROM HIM.

I Gat your *letter,* dainty lad,
    (The fourteenth *ult.* I grant receit;)
Which made me fain right blythe an' glad,
    An' eke a sonnet in your debt.

But man, the bonie lengthen'd day;
    The hedges green, an' flow'ry lee,
With singin' birds on ilka spray,
Hae sta' my *Muse* awa frae me!

In truth, she's turn'd sae vera' wild,
    She'll scrimply tent me whan I speak,
An' scarcely thinks it worth her while
    To board wi' me ance i'the week -

As down a glen I hap'd to wan'er,
    Whar sweet a crystal burnie play'd;
There luckily by chance I fan' her
    Beneath a milk-white hawthorn's shade.

Quoth I, why sittin' here alane?
    Let's hie us hame wi' a' our speed!
An' try ance mair in hamely strain,
    To kittle up the rural reed.

Shall - the wall o' norland chiels,
    Thus gratefu' heeze ye up to fame;
Yet ye'll gay saunterin thro' these fiel's
    Nor min' to thank him for the same!

Sae hame we hied, and in a doop,
    I gets my paper, pen an' ink;
There fla's enow, but yet I hope
    Ye'll at a fellow's *failings* wink -

Your bonie poem that you sent me,
    O! what a heap o' flattery's in't!
Yet 'to the *nines* it did content me!'
    Sae smooth auld-farrant, sleek an' quaint.

O' wit an' sense but sma's my share,
    Tho' whiles I pen a *senseless sang*:
It helps to frighten carkin' care,
    An' keeps mysel frae thinkin' lang.

This while I h' spent in spinnin rhyme,
    An' means in time to mak a buke o't:
An' if it be na' thought a crime,
    I'll gie the *crazy world* a luk' o't.

Now criticks, use me as you will,
    An' at my Musie sklent your spite:
Your censure can do little ill -
    'Twill never hin'er me to write.

Your Grammar chaps may gloom upo' me
    An' ca' me craz'd - but - P - hark! -
Gude L—d I'll try't come what will o' me,
    Tho' I shou'd forfeit coat an' sark!

I'm poet poor as any lark;
    I scarce a shilling can command,
Nor *house* nor *garden, bog* nor *park,*
    As ye may easily understand.

Since no' ae' *spot,* on earth below,
    With justice I can claim as mine;
From place to place I'll musing go,
    And never cast a *wish* behind.

I'll aiblins beg yet - what o' that!
    Auld HOMER did the same lang-syne:
I'll sooth a tune an'never fret,
    Ye ken it's nonsense to repine. -

The grassy glen, - the blooming thorn!
    The purling rill an' flow'ry lee!
Ilk fairy scene on Simmer's morn,
    All nature thro' has sweets for me.

Thoughtless I plod life's giddy maze;
    An' now an' then attune the reed
To rural strains in nature's praise,
    Till Time shall count me with the dead.

Pipe on gay lad, as thou'st begun,
    Henceforth I'll ca' thee friend an' brother:
Glad hand in hand, we'll hie us on,
    An' speel PARNASSUS HILL together.

Now least I might my frien' offend,
    An' wi' my nonsense wrack his brain;
I'll tak a snuff, - fling by my pen,
    An' let my Muse t'her glen again.

May 24, 1791

TO THE SAME

FRAE verdant braes whar gowans bloom,
While Simmer sleeps on hill an' howm;
Again my frien' I thus presume
    Anither sang:
Avaunt ye criticks! here I come,
    Be't right or wrang.

    Come Muse while ilka sunny scene
Is clad in claes o' gayest green;
To him wha has sae aff-han' been,
    Soothe up a lilt:
Tho' right unsnod he'll no complain -
    Haste let us till't.

    The fiel's are co'erd wi' waving corn;
The whispering breezes chear the thorn;
The mist lies laigh at early morn,
    Adown the vales:
Sweet, halsome scents are saftly borne
    Alang the dales.

    In rhyme, I'm proud ye persevere,
But - P - my callan have-a-care!
An' ay o' flattery unco spare,
    'Twere onie matter;
In rhyme ye're witty, slee an' quer;
    But faith ye flatter!

    Ye tell me ye hae got a wife
To share the sours an' sweets o' life:
May ye in geer an' bairns grow rife,
    An' Heaven's bless ye -
A peaceful lot, unknown to strife,
    'S the warst I wiss ye.

Pluck up a heart my lad, an' syne
Your able shou'der lay to mine;
Auld Erin yet we'll mak to shine
    In measur'd pages -
O! had I talents, BURNS like thine,
    I'd sing thro' ages!

Let greedy misers thum' their gowd,
An' gaping clergy bawl aloud,
Whas hearts are aften better stow'd
    Wi' greed than grace,
I'll justle thro' the busy crowd
    Wi' laughin face.

As lang's I'hae paper, pen an' ink,
An' now an' then a gill to drink,
I'll laugh an' dance an' sing an' wink
    At fickle Fortune:
She'll aiblins gie me yet a blink,
    Tho' 'tis uncertain.

Ye Powers! that chauk out each their lot,
Gi'e me (for wealth I value not,)
But health an' claes to turn the wat,
    An' now an' then,
A heart-inspiring, moderate pot
    Wi' honest men.

E'en let the busy, justling warl,
O'er hight and howe 'bout riches quarrel,
For my part I shall never snarl,
    Nor wite the times,
Gin I get gill an' girdle farl,
    An' frien's an' rhymes.

My spunkie blythe, ay whan at leisure,
Let's hae your thoughts in hamely measure,
Which I'll receive wi' meikle pleasure,
　　　An' for your sake,
I'll keep your lines a lasting treasure,
　　　While life's awake.

For ilka verse, my social swankie,
I'se no forget in rhyme to thank ye;
I'll up amang the Bardies rank ye,
　　　In Temple Fame:
Set crously down a dapper shanky -
　　　Ye's hae a Name.

Permit me now, before we part,
To wish the following frae my heart -
May ye ne'er want a foamin' quart,
　　　An' pint an' gill;
A Musie willing, gleg, alert,
　　　An' pliant quill.

May happiness for lang abide,
An' ever wait thy fire-side:
May ye lang out o'er the warl stride,
　　　Wi' healthfu' birr -
Sae now I think ye're fairly paid,
　　　Gude evening, Sir.

June 25, 1791

TO A BLOCKHEAD - AT SCHOOL

O QUIT it, my friend! nor continue so foolish;
Leave learning to those that have genius to polish.
Why thus yourself puzzle 'bout Latin and Greek,
When English you neither can read, write, nor speak?
With Virgil, *et cetera,* no more vex your head;
But if you persist, spite of Nature to read,
With nothing mysterious your intellect numb;
Get Friar and Boy, and the tale of Tom Thumb,
Ballads, and pieces like Jockey and Maggy,
Such innocent merriment never will plague ye.
Tho' faith I would rather advise, as a neighbour,
Quit books altogether, and strike up with labor,
Shake hands with a shovel; a dunghill you'll find,
A subject congenial at once to your mind.

JOHN CRICKET

JOHN CRICKET was a crafty clown,
    An' monie a penny made
Amang the young folk, up and down,
    By fortune-telling trade.

Upon a day, as chance wad hae't,
    In nibour Hab's, the sinner
Would wide display the beuk o' fate,
    Gin they'd gie him his dinner.

To gie his stots the mid-day hire,
    Hab happen'd hame to come,
He saw the prophet at the fire,
    And stepping to the room;

A cricket on a table there,
    Beneath a dish he whumell'd;
"Just now I'll trick this cunning spaer,"
    Thus to himself he mumbled.

He cries on John, wi' angry look,
    An' syne the door secur'd,
An' drew frae out a cobweb neuk,
    A rusty Highland sword:

Now, quoth the farmer, "at a word,
    "Tell what's beneath that dish,
"Or with this guilt-avenging sword,
    "I'll gut you like a fish."

All round and round he ey'd the bowl,
    But naething could discover:
Then bawl'd out with despairing gowl,
    "Alas! poor Cricket's over."

Then Halbert belching out an oath,
   Upon the spaeman gazed,
Remov'd the dish at once, when both
   Were equally amazed.

ON THE DEATH OF A TAYLOR

NOW Heck's awa, the king o' leers,
Wha aft by wicked taunts an' jeers,
Has set together by the ears,
    Douce fok at strife,
Grim Death has clipt wi' his gleg sheers,
    The *thread* o' life!

Death wha the nimblest ay has catch'd,
An' hitherto the strong o'ermatch'd,
Wi a *double thread* his fate has stitch'd,
    'Tis press'd an' grippit,
The mortal sure wad seem bewitch'd,
    Wad try to rip it.

When he the tyrant comin' saw,
He gied his hips the farewell cla'
Then shrugging up a dismal thra'
    Wi' chaps ajar:
His nimble spirit springs awa',
    "It maks na whar."

WILLY SINGS GRIZZY'S AWA

TUNE - "Humours o' Glen."

For I maun own, now since you're free,
This too fond heart o' mine,
Has long, a black-role true to thee,
Wish'd to be pair'd with thine.
RAMSAY

Now fare ye well Grizzy, my bonny wee lady,
  My blessing be wi' ye wherever ye dwell,
But send me back word, and as soon as ye're ready,
  I'll come to ye gladly, and court ye mysel'.

Tak' tent, bonny lassie, and dinna deceive me,
  Lock up your wee bosom, and gie me the key,
And tell the fool hash o' your heart wad bereave ye,
  Ye hae n'it ava, for ye gied it to me.

Ye left it wi' him who took care ay to breed it,
  And guard it frae every thing wicked and vain,
Who gowf'd thy wee buttocks ay when they had need o't,
  Correcting thee kindly, as thou'd been his ain.

How happy I sat by thy elbow when spinning,
  Sae sober and douce, wi' the cat on thy knee;
I thought I foresaw, in thy bonny beginning,
  The sonsy wee auld wife just cut out for me.

But now thou's forsaken our valley sae cheery,
  Where thou had thy time o't, and laughin' galore,
To dwell in a desolate wilderness dreary,
  The heath-cover'd highlands o' wild Dunagore.

And lest my wee lass as she's pensively roaming,
  In that gloomy region should chance to think lang,
Wi' some bonny lilt she maun cheer up the gloaming,
  And let ay mysel' be the theme o' her sang.

While I, her fond Willy, stray thoughtful, recounting
    The blessings that Hope from her habersack teems,
My wishes meet hers on the brow o' the mountain,
    And laden with raptures, come back to my dreams.

But soon as the season wheels round to the short night,
    When meadows are green, and the roddings are dry
I'll come to my jewel ay ance in the fortnight,
    And clasp in my bosom my heart's only joy.

Then sweetly delighted we'll feast on the blisses
    That flow from a rational virtuous love;
When tir'd with talking, I'll tell thee in kisses
    How truly sincere and how constant I'll prove.

Ance mair fare thee weel, my delightfu' wee Grizzy,
    Gae hame to your mammy, and dinna think lang,
May thousands o' vermin till death keep him bisy,
    That ever wad mint your sweet innocence wrang.

Feb. 1804

WILLY'S FAREWELL TO WHISKEY

Strong drink is raging, and doth make
The wisest man a fool,
And he that is deceiv'd thereby,
Is just a senseless mule.
                    SOLOMON'S PROVERBS

WHISKEY, fare you well for ever,
    Brandy, Rum, and Gin likewise;
Never more shall your sad fever,
    Feed on my repenting sighs.

Never more, you may believe me,
    Shall you turn my moon-struck brain,
Priests and Levites now forgive me,
    I will ne'er be drunk again.

Too long, alas! I've prostituted
    Parts, for other purpose given,
Than to babble, all imbruted,
    Wickedly insulting Heaven.

Singin', rantin', roarin', swearin',
    Frae gloaming's close, till breaking day;
Tholing vulgar blockheads' jeerin',
    That kept sober, as they say.

A long farewell to Gib and Beattie,
    M'Adam too, and kind M'Bride,
I'm now resolv'd henceforth to quit ye,
    And for mysel at home provide.

Ye hogs abhorring social riot,
    Scandal mongers he and she,
Now for goodness' sake lie quiet,
    And let poor, fool drinkers be.

I own I oft, thro' human weakness,
  Stept aside, and took my dram,
When, in sp'rit of Christian meekness,
  You were ready still to damn.

I will neither curse nor ban ye,
  Base, calumniating storks,
But as th' apostle said o' Sawney,
  Lord reward ye for your works.

As for you, my hearty fellows,
  That adore the merry squeeze,
To all their filthy jargon callous,
  Drink and sing as long's ye please.

Let Pharisees deride your reeling,
  Poor, conceited, empty smush,
Yours is every generous feeling,
  Truth, and every lib'ral wish.

If that I should chance to pass ye,
  Gaily set - a jovial squad,
Never mind me, gladness bless ye,
  Drinking puts me raving mad.

Howe'er, to make an affidavit,
  Would be farther still astray,
My honest promise here you have it,
  Keep or break it as I may.

Altho' I thus relinquish drinking,
  Random splore, and social noise,
Don't let my old friends be thinking,
  That I am without my joys.

Now when laverocks sing good-morrow,
  To the sun, at early dawn,
Who, that health enjoys, can sorrow,
  Wand'ring o'er the dewy lawn?

Catching every wild-wood rapture,
    Floating on the balmy gale,
Reading his delightful chapter,
    In the fragrant, daisied vale.

Joys are here, worth all their puncheons,
    Joys, that blockheads cannot find;
So farewell whiskey, din and nonsense, -
    Welcome health, and peace of mind.

April 30th 1802

DAVIE AND SAWNEY

AN ALE-HOUSE ECLOGUE

Learn then the best to take from evil,
As Saints take warning by the Devil.

PENROSE

'TWAS on a snell October mornin',
When contra' fok had a' their corn in,
An' northern hills began to shaw
Their heathy summits white wi' sna,
By *chance* or *fate*, it maksna whether,
Davie an *Sawney* met thegither;
Syne after ithers weelfare speering,
To which the muse gied little hearing;
Each having three pence he cou'd spare,
Agreed a wee to bother care,
An' try ae haf hour to be happy,
Out o'er a glass o' reaming nappy.
So to the change house on the hill,
Kent by the sign o' auld *King Will*,
The honest social twasome stepit,
And for a gill o' whiskey chapit:
Which soon as smell'd the spirits rous'd,
An' tongues miraculously lous'd;
Reserve, that hatefu' stumbling block
To the happiness of *sober* fok,
It kick'd aside, while friendship glow'd,
And ilka bosom kindly shew'd.
Blythe on the stoupie Davie glances,
First priev'st, and thus the crak commences.

DAVIE

My frien', I'm glad to see ye cythe
Sae hale, contented like, and blythe;
I was hearing that some turns o' fortune,
The which are at the best uncertain,
Were threat'ning likely to unhorse ye,

An' what I look upon as worse ay,
Some passionate domestic hubbles,
Had flung you 'neath a lade o' troubles.
I hope, however, that a wrangs
Are set to rights, when clatterin' tongues,
That waur than rankest poison kill
Good characters, now rest them still.
Here's peace and plenty t'ye, boy;
If nae ane wish'd ye waur than I,
Grim Calumny wad never crack
Your character behint your back.

                    [*Drinks*]

SAWNEY

Davie, alas! I'll tell you now,
What fok reports is o'er true,
I hae a wife o' Satan's get,
Frae tophet sent to keep me het;
The heaviest losses I hae shar'd
Are light as naithing, when compar'd
To this unfeeling strumpet's clamour -
Her girning and eternal yawmour,
When by my fire I'd rest a wee,
Hath made my house nae hame to me.

DAVIE

That's ae thing in which I am blest;
I hae a wife o' wives the best;
Averse to idleness and strife,
She's just the pillar o' my life.
Tho' sometimes here and sometimes there,
Abroad at market town or fair,
Yet ne'er the less when she's at hame,
A' things are manag'd just the same.
Sae readily as she can rin
About her business, out an' in;
Gude faith I aften ferlie at her,
An' bless my fortune that I gat her.

SAWNEY

Alas, man! I've met the reverse,
An idle waster for a curse;
A noisy torment late and air,
My fortune cast out to my share!
If I'm frae hame, as ye remark,
Instead o' aiding weel the wark,
She steeks the door, and aff she sets,
Bare leggit, to her sister Bet's
The hale day out to lie and clink,
Her neighbours backbite, eat and drink.
The ky at hame may break the dykes,
And eat the corn; the rakin' tykes
Destroy the lambs and eke the hens,
While Peggy neither cares nor kens.
Right wearied, wi' an empty wame,
Full monie a time, when I come hame,
The door I'll get securely locket,
The key's forsooth in Peggy's pocket.
Syne I maun thole till 'bout the glomin,
Till this unfeeling, shameless woman,
Adjourn the clatt'rin, idle din,
An' skelpin come to let me in!
When in, I'll out the fire see,
An' nought ava prepar'd for me.
She'll aiblins say - nae doubt yer hungry,
And frown and stare at me right angry;
So scour out lightly to the byre,
While I, without meat, light or fire,
Wi' care and hunger sore bestead,
In silence graip the way to bed,
Which aft indeed I get unmade.
Syne streek me down, wi' sighs an' tears,
Beseeching Heaven, that never hears,
To order or commission Fate,
To ether end or mend my state.
I oft, in passion, with the jilt,
Ungot, ay, and her father gelt;
For sure nae man was ever vext

Sae—tortur'd, harrow'd, and perplex'd!
Each day brings unexpected losses,
And every week its fretting crosses;
So that, as ye observ'd at first,
I'll soon be weel eneugh unhors'd;
And I sall gie, whan doun I fa'
My wicked wife the wyte of a'.

DAVIE

Trouth, nibour Sawney, I am sorry,
But can, alack, do naething for ye.
I vow an' swear I'd rather lea' her,
Than be thus vex'd and harrass'd wi' her.
Had careful Providence ordain'd
That she'd haen children to maintain'd,
I kenna how, aneath the sin,
Ye cou'd a kept a house within;
A' things are order'd right, and therefore
Nae offspring ye hae got to care for.
But as for me, an' thanks to heaven,
O' a rising family I hae seven;
Four charming lads, an' lasses three,
And better bairns there canna be.
The lasses, I am proud to find,
Possess alike their mither's mind;
While the others manifest already,
The vera temper o' their daddy.
While life-blood heats my Lizie's cheek,
I dinna value fate a leek.
She's just the centre o' my system,
The worth on which account I blest am.
At times whan we together share
A nibour's treat, or simmer fair,
She's ay in sic a kindly wark,
Setting my cravat an' my sark;
My coat to brush, my shoen to hae
As black as ink or onie slae;
Unnotic'd till we be awa,
My hoes she'll able spy a-thra,

She'll quickly speak an' nae them straighted,
And every thing about me righted;
As vera nice I ne'er cou'd be,
She's ay in greater fyke than me;
And says the greatest boast she'll have ay,
Will be to trig the weans and Davie.

SAWNEY

Lang may she bruk baith health and ease,
An' never tint the way to please!
May bitter canker never stare
You i' the face, or gie you care!
But friendly, social, and content ay,
Count monie a day in midst o' plenty!   [*Drinks*]
While I, wi' galling din and strife,
Benumb'd bear up the lade o' life,
Till poverty, in rudest garb,
This tortur'd being quite absorb.
Perhaps kind Providence at length,
When gane are a' my health and strength,
Will nick the thread and gie me rest,
Where poverty nor wives molest.

DAVIE

Ah! Sawney bear, wi' patience wait,
Wha kens how soon relenting fate,
May smooth the path o' comin life,
And to conversion bring your wife?
We read o' Job of early time,
Wha frae prosperity's sublime,
To ruin's vera brink was hurl'd,
And made the bye-word of a world:
Beneath the Devil's brazen paw,
He thol'd, like you, a woman's jaw.
Compar'd to his, what troubles thee,
Is like a dew-drap to the sea;
And yet again he wealthy grew,
So what the duce may hinder you?

The darkest hour o' a' the night
And black, is that before day-light;
These trials sharp to man are given,
That he may better relish heaven.
Be patient man, hope for the better,
Kind heaven may soon amend the matter.
"Then why shou'd we quarrel for riches,
     Or any such glittering toys?
A light heart and thin pair of breeches,
     Will go thro' the world brave boys."

SAWNEY

I ance cou'd sing and rant as weel
As onie ither countra chiel;
To rural glee and social fun,
Cou'd gie my hours frae sun to sun;
At village dance or countra fair,
Was still amang the foremost there;
But now these laughin times are fled,
And troubl'ous days come in their stead;
Henceforth *incog.* I'll try to live,
And out o' sight o' mankind grieve!
Wi' heavy heart an' tear-wet face,
Alone bewail my hapless case.

DAVIE

Come, let us hae anither gill,
An' ance mair, Sawney, tak our fill;
Let hood-wink'd fortune smile or frown,
Tak' aff your glass and sorrow drown;
For whether mortals sigh or sing,
Regardless time is on the wing.
Some row in plenty, some in want,
Some sigh and graen, while ithers rant.
Pure happiness, unmix'd wi' care,
Right sennil visits mankind here.
Be patient Sawney, silly man
Is but a worm, his days a span.

[91]

Thus crack'd the twasome o'er their nappy,
The ane sair griev'd, the ither happy,
Whar nane their converse did o'erhear,
Except the muse, that slyly near
Them sat, hard by, and a' recorded
And brought it hame to get it worded.
Ay whan she eyes the poor man's cot,
She calls to mind his bitter lot;
And frae her cheek, with tender han' ay,
She wipes the tear for luckless Sawney.

LISTEN LIZIE,
LILTING TO TOBACCO.

Now cease your sweet pipes, shepherds; cease your lays
Ye warbling train, that fill the echoing groves
With your melodious love-notes; die ye winds,
That o'er Arcadian valleys blow; ye streams,
Ye garrulous old streams, suspend your course,
And listen "Lizie."

LANGHORNE

TOBACCO dear, attend a wee,
I'm gawn to tune my pipe to thee;
This threty year, I'm sure, and three,
           I hae enjoy'd thee;
Ten times a day, to gie me glee,
           Hae I employ'd thee.

Let ither poets praise the Diel,
Rant, rhyme, an' tipple till they reel,
Or roose potatoes or ait-meal
           In sonnet slee;
Here, hale an' hearty, at my wheel,
           I'll croon to thee.

But och, alas! whan thou wears *short*,
Nae thought hae I for sang or sport;
And neebour loons, that come athort,
           Then like to taunt ay;
Haf deaf, haf blin', my tow I ort,
           And girn and gaunt ay.

An' whan thou'rt out, O *potent weed!*
Our house gaes fairly wrang indeed,
Cogs, pots an' pans fa' arse o'er head,
           An' lie unwashen
An' aften kicks an' licks succeed
           A rash expression.

Our auld gude-man haf tynes his wit,
As by the fire he'll girn an' sit;
His nose an' chin wad mak a nit
          In flinners flee!
Diel haet he dow but girn an spit,
          When wantin thee.

E'en *Colley* shuns the fire-side,
An' *Baudrons* flyt within to bide,
Maun to the stack-yard rin an' hide,
          Or to the kiln,
Else monie a bang does her betide,
          Gien wi' gude will.

But soon as *haf-a-quarter's* come,
Ill nature sinking, maun sing dumb,
That girnin pest that sticks to some
          Fok while they move,
When ilka gab, just like a lum,
          Begins to stove.

Thou hast a wonderful effect
Upon the human intellect;
Can mair than hafflins correct
          Our strife and din,
And passions, wayward things, detect,
          An' haud them in.

Even squalid beggars, cheer'd by thee,
Can sit them down, baith blythe and free,
Just in the shade o' some auld tree,
          Upon their poaks,
Gie ilka care an' pain the lee,
          An' tak' their smoaks.

How hae I leugh a meikle deal,
At thoughtless gowk, frae *cutty stale,*
Puff out great mouthfu's - syne grow pale,
          As onie hawkey;
Sweat, shake, an' bokin', lose his meal,
          Then damn tobacco.

Frae this let ilka raw mou'd slab,
An' geeglin fool, newfangled drab,
Nae mair their squeamish stammacks crab,
                            For by my sang
They'll fin it tak's a season'd gab
                            To thole thee lang.

But by degrees whan yonker tries thee,
Just bit by bit, no to surprise thee,
I'll lay my lugs he gaes and buys thee,
                            Dear as thou art,
And faith he'll never mair despise thee,
                            Nor seek to part.

Wad ilka ragged, tippling hash,
But learn to quat that whisky trash,
An' up wi' thee the matter clash,
                            An' stay at hame,
He'd hain his health an' save his cash,
                            Nor stain his name.

Whan supper's o'er an' our blythe fok,
Aroun' the ingle sit an' joke,
How sweet to tak' our social smoak,
                            An' tell the news;
Discord dare never gie a croak
                            Into the house.

But soon as kittle politicks
Amang our cracks begin to mix,
The settling clouds o' anger fix
                            On every brow;
We curse the wars - wish broken necks,
                            What can we do?

O * * * * * * * * I'll no misca thee,
Nor e'er be heard to say foul fa thee,
But wad auld Hornie arslins draw thee,
                            To his mirk sty,
And there sae curry, nip, an' claw thee,
                            I'd dance for joy.

But why this wicked fool digression!
Why put mysel in sic a passion?
Rebellion's got a pretty thrashin -
                    Sedition's choakin;
When peace returns, we'll thrive in fashion,
                    So let's be smoakin.

Tobacco, monie a whang o' thee,
Has wil'd awa the placks frae me;
What I hae cost for ae bawbee,
                    Now stans me twa;
But siccan times as now we see,
                    We never saw.

An' yet, in spite o' a' their dow,
Auld ERIN will yet in plenty row,
Hae rowth o' thee to smoak I trow,
                    Baith night and day,
Whan monie a wily wicked pow
                    Stinks in the clay.

Some like to snuff thee, some to chow,
While frae their jaws the slavers flow,
Till it wad sconner onie sow,
                    An' poison pigs,
To see their beards a' laggart grow
                    Like sooty wigs!

An wives, forsooth, wi' nebs like snipes,
Stan' out frae cheeks, like scrapit tripes,
Snievel an' dreep, but onie wipes,
                    Save on their cuff -
Might gie a Highlandman the gripes
                    At takin snuff.

Since chewing thus your jaws exposes,
An' snuff makes tar-pigs o' yer noses;
Since smoakin breaks nae law o' Moses,
                    Come seat you free,
Lug out your pipe, fill'd up *jocusus*,
                    An' smoak wi' me.

As some day soon I mean to tak' a
Day, to sing to thee Tobacco,
Some dainty lilt that fok' may crack o';
                         Gin't dinna miss,
Thou'lt suffer me, but words to mak' a
                        Tail end to this.

Now musie light, an' rest thy wing,
While I fall slack the merry string,
And up the canty fiddle hing,
                        Syne we sall tak' a,
Hearty smoak - an' close the spring,
                        Wi' hail TOBACCO.

POSTSCRIPT

WITH A POUND OF SNUFF

TAKE not, my dear Sir, my present amiss,
You may open at once and see what it is:
Or I'll tell you in short tho' I merit a cuff,
'Tis a pound of the best of *old Lundy Foot's* snuff;
'Tis B——d they call it, I'm told in the city,
'Mong people of fashion that fain wou'd be witty;
But here in the north, we call it *Rappee:*
D——l sniffle the odds! there's a pound o't to thee.

I sent for't to Dublin, an' mist it - at last
I heard that I might have a *pound* in Belfast:
I ask'd for a *sample* before that he weigh'd it,
The old fellow swore by the L——d he cou'd eat it;
I try'd it so rash, - set my opticks a springing;
It stichel'd me so that I straight fell a singing -
Here take it, an' use it, an G——d gie ye gude o't,
An' may it inspire your Muse, if it cou'd do't,
In bonie *braid Scotch* to sing me a sonnet,
On receipt of which, I would dance on my bonnet:
I'd rather I vow, than a ton o' sic *priming,*
That I had your *musical talents* for rhyming!
In the mean time gude night, an' may Providence bless ye, -
Ye'd no be ill-fair'd if as weel as I wiss ye.

Carngranny, near Belfast,
18th April, 1792

ELEGY, TO MY AULD COAT

NOW fare you weel my honest frien'!
This monie a long spun day ye h' been
To my *outside* a sonsy screen
    Frae weet and cauld;
An' monie a *social hour* I h' seen
    Aneath your fauld.

    Ye war ance a colour fresh an' fair,
An shap'd in *fashion* to a hair;
But now ye're auld an' grown thread-bare
    Frae sleeve to skirt;
Alack! it wrings my bosom sair,
    That we maun part.

    Wi' you exulting monie a time,
High up a stride on thought sublime,
I h' trac'd the flow'ry fiel's o' rhyme,
    Aneath Apollo;
An' made t' the winds my ditties chyme
    O'er height an' hollow!

    Let the ungratefu' thoughtless loon,
Gae prostitute his *coat* when done,
To office vile, o' cleaning shoen,
    Or what's far waur;
Hing't up some barley rig aboon,
    The craws to scaur!

    Unlike to him, I'll lay ye by,
In some lee corner, snug an' dry,
Whaur ye may rest, while duly I
    Shall turn an' air ye;
For 'till the dreary day I die
    I'll ay revere ye.

ELEGY, TO MY AULD SHOEN

ADIEU my pumps, your days are done;
Ah wae is me, your race is run!
Now to the mools, my worthy shoen,
    I'm forc'd to send ye!
The cobler has declar'd ye gone -
    He canna' mend ye!

    Tho' yet I shall be laith to scorn ye,
O'er monie a moss and moor ye've born me,
An' monie a lang an' dreary journey
    Baith late, an' soon,
Thro' days an' nights cauld, wat an' stormy,
    But now ye're done.

    I'll say't, great pains I took alway,
To gie ye baith alike fair play:
I chang'd ye duly ilka day
    I pat ye on;
But now, gude faith I'm e'en right wae,
    To see ye done.

    Three quarters now are near han' past,
Sin that night ye cam aff the last;
Ye never gat an hour's rest,
    Save whan I slept:
Mair honest stuff was never drest
    O' cawf or kip.

    Nae mair my social hours ye'll dree;
Nae mair ye'll scour the daisied lee;
Nae mair to dance ye'll carry me,
    Nor ever mair
Those happiest of my minutes see
    Beside my fair.

But why shou'd I at fate repine?
'Tis just the same wi a' man kin':
Then let us a' to heaven resign;
    For, like our shoen,
From lifes meridian we decline
    Until we're done.

THE BONNET - A POEM

ADDRESSED TO A REVEREND MISER

(*Advertisement*)

Ye wha hae seen hell's horned knight,
Sough owre a midnight brae,
Can only boast o' sic a sight
As I saw yesterday.

The following Poem, if such it may be called, had a curious
fact for its foundation. A certain Rev. Gentleman, better
known by the singularity of his dress than a liberal or
charitable disposition, happening on the afternoon of a warm
day, in the month of July, one year, to be out, either on a soul-
saving or hunger-destroying excursion, passed the Author's
door in the following trim, which curious sight gave rise to
the rhyme:- Old black stocking-legs partly conceal'd his shins;
by this t'will be understood his feet were bare; a pair of blue
linen breeches, unbuttoned at the knees, worn, rip'd, tatter'd
and torn, hung over his Rev. buttocks; a waistcoat of the same
cloth with the breeches, but so miserably reduced that one
might conceive even the ragman would refuse, unbuttoned,
hung on his shoulders. He had on no coat. Let us not forget
to render justice to his careful wash-woman, he had on a very
well done up shirt.

But what crowned all, was his head incased in a
woman's black bonnet! As his back, apparently more from the
negligence of Nature in his formation, than the effect of a
burden of years, is wonderfully bent - even an unthinking
stranger may figure to himself this ludicrous picture. To such
as have the honour and happiness to live in the same
neighbourhood with the Gentleman, this *rude draught* will be
altogether superfluous. I fondly hope, however, that the
singularity of the sight will plead my apology with both those
that know him and those that do not. I know, as a worthy
Author has said, "That Corbies and Clergy are a shot right
kittle;" but Nature, in her freaks, hath given me such a
tickleness of intellect, that when I accidentally, or otherwise,

meet with any thing risible in itself, even tho' I should be guillitined for it, 'tis altogether out of my power to keep from laughing.

"Not laugh? beasts, fishes, fowls, nor reptiles can,
That's the peculiar privilege of man."

THE BONNET

*For **that** (quoth he) let me alone,*
We've store of such, and all our own,
Bred up and tutor'd by our teachers,
The ablest of conscience-stretchers.

HUDIBRAS

HA! —— —— Whar got ye that?
Whar hae ye flung th' ald wool hat?
Hae ye hung't up, being auld and torn,
To fright the rooks frae 'mang the corn,
Or thrown't in spider neuk, to lig
Alang wi' th' auld rejected wig?
Tho' scoff'd and hol'd, depend upon it,
Ye set it better than a bonnet.
Perhaps some loon your absence watches,
And short repasts of pleasure snatches;
And, while stern Jealousy plants her thorns,
Ye clap on this to hide the horns.
Perhaps ye think, an' ye're nae goose,
This keeps your *Craneum* brave and loose;
While that a hat confines the same,
And ideas get owre het at hame.
Reverse o' these auld brainless bodies,
Wha drone a' day in dusky studies;
With energy of mind possest,
When labouring out ye study best;
An' can contrive in a dyke sheugh,
What may do poor fok weel enough.

Being fond to keep, to latest date,
Your *colour,* at the cheapest rate,
(Tho' ane might trow, to see your buff,
It might amaist be weather proof.)
This *cowl* prevents the staring *sin,*
Frae with'ring up your cheek an' chin.
Unlike these *Macaroni* fellows,
Wha, flaunting, spread their *umberellas,*
Tripping, tip toe, in gaudy claithing,
While, save what's on them, they hae naithing;
Naithing at hame, but empty bags:
Ye store the gowd an' gang in rags!
I've heard ye mair than ance or twice
Assert that all extremes were vice;
If so, your R——— is to blame,
O'er head and ears is *one extreme!*
But stiff-neck still, you seem to think,
That first an' foremost - meat an' drink,
And any kind of thread-bare clothing,
Not bought I mean, but got for nothing,
Are all that's needful, straight or crooked,
And gold was made - for what? to look at.
While from your *rostrum* you deride
All ostentation, pomp and pride,
Ah! on yourself cou'd you but look,
And see as you see other fok',
Ye'd see your humped back support
A turse of pride of other sort.
For pride exists in monie a form;
And surely there's as little harm
In that which trips in fashion nice,
As that which creeps in rags and lice.
As matron Nature has took pains
On nought about you but the brains,
L—d, Sir, you shou'd be more exact!
The million tauk behint your back;
Your shape, resembling Hudibrases,
You render worse by these odd dresses;
With an old wife's bonnet on your pow,
You'd fright the pigs from any sow.

Twad much amend the matter, faith,
Wad ye but gang in decent claith.

    Although at you and your apparel,
'Tis impudence in me to snarl;
But when I see, wi' auld or young,
Aught odd, I canna had my tongue.
Your graceless flock are grown sae lazy,
An' lukewarm, they have put you crazy;
In tresspasses and sins, they're dead;
For you they'll neither drive nor lead!
While like a tug you wingle wi' them,
Unwilling to be sun'er'd frae them;
When fleechin winna do, ye'll even
Attempt to frighten them to heaven!
To pass the *cot* (craving your pardon)
Ye ken'd there woun'd a bleth'rin bard in,
Wha keeks, *incog.* at man an' woman,
An' whan he meets wi' aught uncommon,
In hamely, aff hand, rural rhymes,
Sends all in print to future times;
For you, I say, to pass his *dore*,
In siccan garb, mad-like as Caor,
Your R—— was a little out,
You might, he thinks, have gone about.

    'Twas mercy, Sir, wi' siccan hood on,
Nae breeding wife met you the road on!
If onie had, I'll tak my aith,
Far less has been a woman's death.

    Perhaps ye read this fellow's book,
An' there observ'd nae note is took
Of you - ye thought, ance for a joke,
Ye'd try his *musie* to provoke,
And, right or wrong, to future ages,
Shine on his next edition's pages;
And so ye shall, dear R—— ——
Thro comin' times, wi' bonnet on ye,
Link it alang like *countra* carline,

While gaping rustics will be ferlying,
Taking ye for the witch of En-dor,
(L—d save's!) or some sic like pretender.

Gude faith, ye'll aiblins tak' it ill,
That I hae thus employ'd my quill
On you, and your concern - but shud ye
E'en gar me girn for't thro' a widdie,
To see you wi' a bonnet skelp it,
O L—d, my sire, I could not help it!

But gin ye be a holy brither,
When ae cheek's smit, ye'll turn the ither,
An' owre this hamely sonnet smile;
To rage is never worth your while.
I fain wad think ye'll no be wroth;
'Tis surely wholesome as sour broth,
The which, 'twas said, you us'd to love,
As cook-maid yet can fairly prove.
She's aftan tauld, that if ye hame
At evening came, with empty wame,
Ye were like a blood-hound or a tiger,
Till sour broth sav'd frae heated beggar,
Wi' pratoes cauld, allay'd the smart
O hunger knawin at your heart;
Or thick or thin, 'twas all the same,
Coarse things do weel eneugh at hame.

Sin' that day's night that ye sae stark,
Had executed three men's wark,
Ye h' lost, alack! your popularity,
An' fa'n amaist beneath vulgarity.
Don't let your R—— think I flaw;
The following fact will clearly shaw,
And corroborate, to your aversion,
Th' existing truth of my assertion.
Suppose to pomp and carry clashes,
Is wark for wicked, graceless hashes;
But if examples we can spy,
Frae sic as you spontaneous fly,

To tell a random clash or *lee,*
Might aiblins be let go free!

   The ither night, as I was wa'kin
About the dykes, I heard twa' ta'kin
Behint a bush; I kept frae view,
And heard what follows - about you!

[*Here, as Tom Gray says, 500 stanzas are lost.*]

Thus, Sir, you see I am not jestin;
But wha was't spake o't? - there's the question:
And not withstanding how I can, Sir,
'Tis one I am not bound to answer:
Full likely 'tis exaggeration,
Or diabolic defamation,
That falsely has supplanted truth,
And prostitues each meddling mouth.
Be't as it will, your R—— may
Dependence put in this I say;
There's several gentles - fok o' fashion,
That oft hae pang'd you like a cushion,
Wha wi' the Devil would rather share
Their conversation and their fare.
If I, as you were haf as able,
To keep an independent table,
I'd see my guts about a thorn,
Before I shou'd incur their scorn,
In any such a low-liv'd way,
Haunting them for their *draps o' tea!*
I kenna whether ye hae took note
O this that I am gawn to quote;
But whether ye hae observ'd or no,
I'm sure I always found it so.
While we conveniently can get
But keeping out o' great fok's debt,
Accepting nought but what we find
We can again return in kind,
Ay whan we meet them, fitch the beaver,
This is the way to win their favor.

But twice or thrice a week or so,
Gude faith we'll from a burden grow,
While from the vera *flunkie's* face,
Sour looks will soon explain the case.

Now Sir, lest I be thought too rude
And impudent, I will conclude:
While ——'s your name, may heaven bless ye;
And earth in better cloathing dress ye;
May your saul ne'er sink to sooty hell,
But ye can pray for that yoursell.
Your patience yet, an inch or twa;-
Just ae word ere I gang awa:
Ken whether ye occupy your wit,
To rail at me an' all I h' writ;
Wrathfu' misca' me, stamp and stare,
Keep up your nieves, I dinna care.
Believe me, Sir, your fist or rung
Wad hurt me far waur than your tongue.
Hencefoth I'll watch an' no gae near ye,
And then I need na muckle fear ye -
Keep that auld bonnet frae my view,
And pray for me, I'll sing for you.

TO MY BOORTREE

WRITTEN AT THE DESIRE OF THE REV MR C———

AULD Maro, wha sae weel could teach
Sublimity's mount tap to reach,
Was glad his lusty limbs to stretch
        And coil his rod, *
Beneath the shelter o' a beech,
        Upon the sod.

As Poets a' pretend to flee,
Which some hae done right merrily,
Ilk ane sinsyne must have his tree
        To speel and spring aff;
A Boortree's good enough for me
        Howe'er, to sing of.

Flourish my Boortree fresh and fair,
Right monie a holy, well-meant prayer,
John Lowes' grannum put up there
        Upon thy roots,
Whar thae twa suckers, lucky pair,
        Erect their snouts.

What tho' thou'll ne'er be sic a tree
As Billy Shakespeare's mulberry,
Nor e'er ayont the parish be
        A thing to brag on,
'Tis better, for the auld folk, slee,
        Might ca' thee Dagon.

Here blithe beneath thy auld grey branches,
Where sparrows chirp, and spotted finches
Prepare for their companion wenches
        The nest well feather'd;
I bind my wild flowers up in bunches,
        That I hae gather'd.

* *Virgil made baskets.*

Lang syne, in happy days o' yore,
Ere glaring guilt our system tore,
Auld Orthodoxy blest our shore
        Wi' light and grace,
And Boortrees every yard-dyke bore
        In every place.

But now, alas! the generality,
Sad figures of poor man's mortality,
And eke o' poor, decayed morality,
        Are gouk-nest lumber,
Where bats, and ither drowsy quality
        Repair to slumber.

Could we, as our forefathers, meek,
Afford them earth, and *peace,* and *reek,*
Nae ither nourishment they'd seek;
        But och, alas!
Our blasted Boortrees now bespeak
        Our want o' grace!

And then our modern gentry's taste
Up in the devil's whalebone lac'd,
Wad rather own a desert waste,
        O'ergrown wi' rushes,
As hae their puny plans disgrac'd
        Wi' boortree bushes.

Flourish my Boortree fresh and fair,
Long may'st thou Summer's livery wear;
Tho' modern delicacy stare
        Wi' face awry.
Before my door I'll guard thee there,
        Until I die.

VERSES,

ON THE ASSASSINATION OF A FAVOURITE THORN.

> *O deed of sacrilege! in Tophet bred,*
> *To violate the mansions of the dead!* *

O DESOLATION! haggard thing,
    Thou bang-beggar of fools,
Of harpy note and raven wing,
    Curs'd even by thy tools.

Thy black assassins have been here,
    O burn, them, blushing shame!
Remorse their guilty bosoms tear,
    Till they confess the same.

Ah! woe betide the cruel heart
    Wherein such thoughts could breed,
And from the hands may strength depart,
    That did the murdering deed.

And never may their farms appear,
    Till *they* to graves are borne,
The sacred, vernal blooms to wear,
    Of either ash or thorn.

Farewell, gay bush! no more in green,
    Shall Spring be proud to dress thee,
Nor Fairy folk on Halloween,
    In merry mood caress thee.

No more thou'lt spread thy arms to face
    Cold Winter's frost and snow;
Nor ever more in June's embrace,
    Thy milk-white mantle show.

* *It was the request of the present occupier's*
predecessor to preserve this Thorn from violence.

No more shall Autumn, sultry, hot,
    Thy glowing beauty freckle;
But soon beneath some poor man's pot,
    Thy mangled parts must crackle.

The harmless Dryads long since fled
    From yonder ruined grove,
All in distress, found here a shed,
    A fairy-form'd alcove;

But Ruin's persecuting hand,
    Expert at doing ill,
Has left them all a weeping band,
    To wander where they will.

O come away with me fair maids,
    You shall protection have
In yonder lowly, happy shades,
    That shelter Crambo Cave.

There spreading planes and ashes tall,
    Broom, larch, and thorns a store;
A boortree, chaplain-like to all,
    Stands just before my door.

There you may sweetly take your ease,
    Disturb you shall I never;
Your lease shall last, long as you please,
    The Muse declares, for ever.

PASTORAL ELEGY,

TO A FAVOURITE THORN, ON ITS BEING CUT DOWN.

RETURN my muse, and with thee bring
The dowy strains o' sorrowing!
    Alack! and well-a-day!
My thorn that erst sae fresh and green,
Upon yon blank to nod was seen,
    Now ligs among the clay.

Assist me woody minstrels a',
In dowie wise your whistles bla'
    Ye herds across the lee:
Come sing in mournful strains forlorn,
This *bush,* this much lamented *thorn,*
    That was sae dear to me!

To yonder corner turn your e'en,
Then sign and sob an' mourn bedeen,
    And pray that on his head
A ten-fold vengeance hourly fa',
And harpies fell his riggin cla',
    That did the ruthless deed!

Full twenty annual *suits* I've seen
Upon thy sprays, o' gayest green,
    With blossoms white as sna';
Whar busy bees would daily come,
And eager cling with drowsy hum,
    To drain thy sweets awa.

The robin red-breast (serious ay)
With strains o' mournfu' melody,
    A top a neighbouring tree,
Does dowie chant thy obsequies,
Whilst disappointed zephyr sighs
    Alang the sorrowing lee.

Here fairy tribes, bedight in green,
Beneath the moon wad aft convene,
      To gambol, sport and dance:
Whilst ither some, on ragweed naigs,
Out o'er the yellow braes, an' craigs
      Would nimbly wheeling prance.

Na mair the *cuckow* frae thy spray,
With softening note at early day,
      Shall woo the western gale -
Nae mair the *thrush*, wi' monie a note,
Shall stain her downy, tuneful throat,
      Nor linnets lay preval.

Nae mair shall I at e'enin's hour,
Glad hie me to thy peaceful bower,
      A *musing hour* to pass;
To lift the music o' the wood
And watch the playfu' lambies scud
      Alang the velvet grass.

When wint'ry Boreas snelly blaws
Out o'er the fields the drift an' snaws,
      An' nature's face deforms;
Nae mair thy gratefu' breast will yield
To chittering tribes a frien'ly bield,
    A' Shelter frae the storms.

At e'en, when wan'ring frae my cot,
With heavy heart I view the spot -
      The ance ah! pleasing shade;
Where I full oft, in grass-lined chair,
To smooth the wrinkl'd brow o' care,
      My *rural music* play'd.

Whilst I, as heretofore can see
A glimmering blink wi' reason's e'e,
      Remembrance ilka morn,
With dowie muse will carefu' trace,
An dolefu' hing o'er yonder place
      Where stood the sacred *thorn*.

SIMKIN,

OR A BARGAIN'S A BARGAIN - A TALE

A wit's a feather, and a chief's a rod,
But an honest man's the noblest work of God.

POPE

AULD *Sim* was fam'd for prolix prayers,
    And *tuneful* holy graces;
Weel ken'd at markets, mills and fairs,
    And ither public places.

A holy man - his conscience ne'er
    Wad suffer him to curse;
But saftly whisper'd in his ear,
    That he might jockey horse.

He held it as a crying sin,
    At hame, or onie place,
To tak a morsel, thick or thin,
    Without a formal grace.

This favorite o' Heaven ae day,
    To a neighbouring fair wad gang:-
Favourite of Heaven, did I say?
    Gude faith I'm aiblins wrang.

Howe'er his Bawsay to the fair,
    Took crafty, sleekit Sim:
A noble naig he did declare,
    But didna answer him.

Soon up there comes a jockey chiel,
    Sim like a Levite winked;
He tried the horse and lik'd him weel,
    And soon a bargain clinked.

Quoth Sim - "although I say't mysel,
    I'm reckon'd something clever ay;
We'll step in here an tak a gill,
    An' then yese get delivery."

They call'd a gill, 'twas quickly there,
    The chiel gets't in his nieve,
When Simkin, with a holy air,
    Says, 'stranger wi' yer leave.'

Thrice he gov'd up niest the roof,
    As aften shook his head,
Then clos'd his ein, an' rais'd his loof,
    A holy man indeed!

The tricky callan, then, to keep
    Frae laughin scarcely fit,
Drank out the whiskey every seep,
    And down the bicker set.

The grace being done, the fellow leugh,
The whiskey was away!
To pray, quoth he, is not eneugh,
    Hereafter watch and pray.

Delivery gien - they part aff han,
    So hame our nibour wan'ers:
Niest morn the o'erseen fellow fan'
    His gelding had the glan'ers!

Neglecting to ask Simkin's name,
    He's in an eirie study:
At length in passion aff he came,
    Damning the *praying body!*

At lang and length he found the place,
    Our Simkin's habitation;
Where entering in he kend his face,
    And baul'd aloud - damnation!

Ye old infernal hound of hell!
    Ye hypocrite deceiver!
A gland'red horse to me to sell -
    Swith the money up deliver.

'Hooly,' quo Simkin, unco slee,
    'Gie o'er sic sinfu' jargon;
Nae money ye shall get frae me -
    A bargain's ay a bargain.

SONG

JENNY at yon hedge o' broom,
    For Jockey waited lang;
The soughin' blast blew o'er her head
    While thus the maiden sang.
'Thou broom that form'd the dear lov'd shade,
    Where first he vow'd his love;
Say what will come o' me poor maid,
    If Jockey faithless prove?'
        CHORUS - Thou broom &c.-

What hauds my bonie Jockey sae?
    He promis'd he wad come,
And meet his only Jenny here,
    Amang the blooming broom.
The sun's now set an' cauld an' stiff
    The unwelcome gale does bla',
An' black, alang the dewy fiel's,
    The nightly shaddows fa'.
        CHORUS - Thou broom &c.-

There's something ails my bonie lad,
    Or he wad sure been here:
He never us'd to tarry sae;
    There's something wrang I fear!
Cauld an' wat the night will bla',
    The tempest rock the grove:
When I am forc'd within to stay
    An' disappoint my love.
        CHORUS - Thou broom &c.-

Sweet the May-day zephyr bla's
    Alang the flow'ry lee!
But sweeter far than spring's soft gales,
    Is Jockey's breath to me!
Sweet the bloom of summer's role
    Upon her thorny tree!
But sweeter far in smiles array'd
    Is Jockey's face to me!
        CHORUS - Thou broom &c.-

The locks of autumn, waving o'er,
    Delight the careful hind;
But raptures far surpassing such,
    I with my shepherd find.
Tho' rural swains on vernal braes,
    Pipe soft, sweet, artless airs;
There's something in my Jockey's sang,
    That far surpasses theirs.
        CHORUS - Thou broom &c.-

And tho' each shepherd's ruddy face
    Engaging saftness wears:
There's something in my Jockey's look,
    That far surpasses theirs.
Then haste thee bonie shepherd! haste,
    Thy Jenny waits alane:
Ah! Jockey can'st thou laugh an' sing,
    An' let her wait in vain!
        CHORUS - Thou broom &c.-

Ah silly maid the hollow gale,
    Wild whistling thro' the broom,
Bears to thy ear th' unwelcome tale,
    That Jockey canna come.
Thou broom that form'd the dear-lov'd shade
    Where first he vow'd his love;
Say what will come o' me poor maid?
    If Jockey faithless prove.
        CHORUS - Thou broom &c.-

EPITAPHS

ON A. B——

HERE lies beneath this mouldering sod,
Him who the *Paths of Virtue* trod:
Who by affliction's galling rod
      Was early driven -
Whose soul exalted with its God,
        Now dwells in Heaven.

ON SARAH B——

BENEATH this stane - lies Sarah B——
Whose days were spent - in *sin* an' scoffin';
A strap o' strife - a wicked wife -
Now Death has pent - her in a coffin!

ON A PEDLAR,

WHO WAS KILLED AND BURIED ON A HILL.

HERE lies alone, in this wild, cauld place,
O' Pedlar John the luckless *saul-case:-*
When the last trumpet's awfu' blast
Awakes the dead frae silent rest,
He'll start an' stare! - see but himsel' man,
An' call to min' his pack an' ell-wan'.

ON A GUDE FELLOW

HERE R—— rests, an honest weaver,
Wha liv'd an died a droughy b'liever:
A better never threw a shuttle,
Nor empty'd yet, an ale-wife's bottle
For Fortune's frowns - he ay defy'd them,
An' prayin' means - he never try'd them;
Still took the world as it cam',
Laugh'd, jok'd, an sung, an' quaff'd his dram;
But Death in earnest cam' at last,
An' flung him here to tak' his rest.

ON AULD JOSIE

AH Reader! view with tear-wet eye,
The SPOT where Josie's corps do lie -
Thro' life he was a canty carl,
But death has kick'd him from the world.

ON J—— D——

HERE Johny sleeps aneath the storms,
As soun's a tap in Death's cauld arms:
The *shell* is only hidden here -
The *kernels* fled the L—d knows where!

ON A REMARKABLE LITTLE, ILL-FAVOUR'D BODY

HERE lies deserted by the soul,
The clay contents of —— the croul:
He was, —— but now he's dead as mutton,
A M——r, L——r, and a - Gl——n.

EPIGRAM

TO speak the *truth,* an' just nae mair,
Wad fok at ilka time agree;
    At *Kirk* an' *Market, Mill* an' *Fair.*
How modest might our meetings be!

    Were this in time to be the case,
Our *Lawyers* might lay by their tongues:
    Our *Clergy* too, wi' *Solemn Face,*
Might rarely hain their breath an' lungs!

EPIGRAM

Our mother Church, in days of old,
Had oaken *caups* and priests of gold;
But now, with sorrow be it spoken,
Her *caups* are gold, her priests are oaken.

EPIGRAM - TO A READING PREACHER

With formal pomposity, how you can read,
    But meddlers scoffingly mock it;
For sermons, they say, there's no room in your head,
    So you bear them about in your pocket.

From your pocket it comes, but the hearer must pay,
    For the pocket-bred, pitiful jargon;
And, grumbling, at close of the year, he will say,
    Devil take such a profitless bargain.

LINES

*Composed for a stone, intended to be placed in front
of the Rev John Paul's new meeting house, now
building in Carnmoney, 1806*

To show the world that God respects
His covenant, full dear,
The Reformation Church erects
This Ebenezer here.

"Hitherto hath the Lord help'd us."

*And long may he continue to do so, is, and ought
to be the fervent prayer of every good man.*